Copyright ©

ISBN 978-0-915545-23-0

First Printing 2014

Printed in the United States of America
All Rights Reserved!

Published by
Stanley R. Abbott Ministries, Inc.
P.O. Box 533
McRae, Georgia 31055
U.S.A.

Rewards of Heavenly Submission

Preface

If *"...submission..."* is of God, we need to embrace it! If it is of the devil, we need to reject it! Simple! The challenge is having accurate revelation of submission. Without accurate revelation of submission from God's perspective how will we know whether to embrace it or reject it?

The new covenant is a faith based covenant. We are saved *"...by grace through faith..." (**Ephesians 2:8**)*, and we are designed to *"...walk by faith, not by sight..." (**II Corinthians 5:7**)*. New Testament *"...faith comes by hearing, and hearing by the word of God..." (**Romans 10:17**)*. That is, the foundation for our faith is accurate knowledge of God! If we lack accurate revelation of God and the components of His kingdom, it will be impossible to have and exercise *"...faith..."* to live successfully in His kingdom.

We must consider *"...submission..."* in order to determine whether it is of God or not! Only after revelation has been gained and understood will we be able to choose correctly. The purpose for this book is not to *"...persuade..."* you but to present the revelation of *"...submission..."* from a Scriptural base and allow you to see clearly for yourself.

Rewards of Heavenly Submission

Table of Contents

Chapter One
Submission Defined   1 - 10

Chapter Two
From Submission to Un-Submission   11 - 22

Chapter Three
Submission Between Believers   23 - 32

Chapter Four
Jesus' Submission to His Father   33 - 42

Chapter Five
Diversity of Submission   43 - 54

Chapter Six
Submission to Governing Authorities   55 - 68

Chapter Seven
Submission to Spiritual Authorities   69 - 78

Chapter Eight
Submission in Marriage   79 - 94

Conclusion   95 - 97

Chapter One

Submission Defined

Through the course of recorded history there have been many despots or tyrants who desired to rule men. Most such men have pursued their objective by force without consideration for the people they desired to rule. This *subjugation* or *rule-by-force* is anathema within the church of today!

> ***subjugation*** - to subdue and bring under the yoke by superior force
>
> <u>*Webster's New Universal Unabridged Dictionary*</u>

Satan desires to rule men, too, but his methods are typically subtlety and cunning craftiness *(II Corinthians 11:3)*. He endeavors to seduce men with enticements *(1185 James 1:14)* in an effort to allure them into his rule *(James 1:13-15; Romans 6:16)*. Seduction and enticements are what he used in the wilderness in his failed attempt to rule Christ *(Luke 4:1-13)*.

> ***entice*** *1185 deleazo from the base of 1388; to entrap, i.e. (fig.) delude: -- allure, beguile, entice.*
>
> <u>***Strong's Exhaustive Concordance of the Bible***</u>
>
> ***entice*** - *to lead on by exciting hope of reward or pleasure; to tempt*
>
> <u>*Webster's New Universal Unabridged Dictionary*</u>

Rewards of Heavenly Submission

Jesus is ordained to rule men! When God the Father raised Jesus from the dead, He *"...seated Him far above every name that is named..." (Ephesians 1:21)* and willed that *"...in all things Jesus may have the preeminence..." (Colossians 1:18)*!

> ### *It is the will of God the Father for Jesus to rule!*

Jesus' destiny to rule includes *"...head over the church, which is His body..." (Ephesians 1:13-23; Colossians 1:9-18)*, *"...far above all principality and power and might and dominion, and every name that is named, not only in this age but also in that which is to come..." (Ephesians 1:13-23; Colossians 1:9-18)*, *"...King of Kings, and Lord of Lords..." (Revelation 17:14; 19:16)*. According to Scripture a time will come when Jesus' rule will involve a *"...rod of iron..." (Psalms 2:8,9; Revelation 2:18-29)*. However, this type of rule is reserved for another dispensation different from the one in which we now live.

Until the dispensation changes no aspect of Jesus' *"...rule over men..."* involves *"...a rod of iron..."* and **never** involves subtle and crafty enticements in any dispensation. Although Jesus is certainly superior over any and all men, He has chosen not to exert *"...control..."* over men. Nor does He seduce men with enticements designed to allure them into His rule. In order for Jesus to rule men, men must *"...submit..."* to Him based on their knowledge of Him!

Submission Defined

> *In this dispensation Jesus' rule over men requires men's submission!*

What is submission? The actual term *"...submission..."* is not used in the New Testament, but the term *"...submit..."* is. The Greek term is *"...hupotasso..."* listed as number *5293* in <u>Strong's Exhaustive Concordance of the Bible</u>.

> **5293 hupotasso** from *5259* and *5021*; to *subordinate*; reflex. to *obey*: -- be under obedience (obedient), put under, subdue unto, (be, make) subject (to, unto), be (put) in subjection (to, under), submit self unto.

The online source http://www.biblestudytools.com/lexicons/greek/kjv/hupotasso.html provides additional understanding of the term *"...hupotasso..."* based on <u>The KJV New Testament Greek Lexicon by Thayer and Smith</u>...

> "...a Greek military term meaning "...to arrange [troop divisions] in a military fashion under the command of a leader...". In non-military use, it was "...a voluntary attitude of giving in, cooperating, assuming responsibility, and carrying a burden...".

Since there is no *"...rod of iron..."* in Jesus' rule in this dispensation, we can apply <u>Strong's</u> definition of *"...submit..."*, and establish a simple definition of *"...submission..."* in the church as:

> **Submission** *is simply a person's willingness to yield to the rule of Christ.*

Rewards of Heavenly Submission

Why would anyone submit to the rule of Jesus? The role from which God the Father destined Jesus to rule points us in the right direction. God the Father destined Jesus to rule as **Lord** *(Acts 2:32-36)*. The revelation of Jesus as **Lord** is the cornerstone around which the entire church is built *(I Peter 2:1-10)!* Salvation itself is predicated on the **Lordship** of Christ! In other words, God has chosen Jesus as **Lord** to be the doorway through which a person must pass to be saved!

> *"If you will confess with your mouth the Lord (2962) Jesus and believe in your heart that God has raised Him from the dead, you will be saved. For with the heart one believes unto righteousness, and with the mouth confession is made unto salvation. For the Scripture says, 'Whoever believes on Him will not be put to shame.' For there is no distinction between Jew and Greek, for the same Lord (2962) over all is rich to all who call upon Him..."* **Romans 10:9-12**

> **2962 kurios** from *kuros* (*supremacy*); *supreme* in authority, i.e. (as noun) *controller*; by impl. *Mr.* (as a respectful title): -- God, Lord, master, Sir.
>
> <u>**Strong's Exhaustive Concordance of the Bible**</u>

The verses immediately following **Romans 10:9-12** provide additional information regarding a person calling on Jesus as **Lord**.

> *"...For whoever calls on the name of the Lord (2962) shall be saved. How then shall they call on Him in whom they have not believed? And how shall they believe in Him of whom they have not heard? And how shall they hear without a preacher? And how shall they preach unless they are sent? As it is written:*

Submission Defined

> *'How beautiful are the feet of those who preach the gospel of peace, who bring glad tidings of good things!'*
>
> *But they have not all obeyed the gospel. For Isaiah says, 'Lord, who has believed our report?' So then faith comes by hearing, and hearing by the word of God."*
> **Romans 10:13-17**

Here the Holy Spirit inspired written revelation of pre-requisites necessary for a person to be able to call on the ***Lord*** for salvation. The pre-requisites are *"...sending, preaching, hearing, and believing..."*. All of these actions involve people to people. The goal of these actions is to make Jesus known so a person may have opportunity to call on Jesus as ***Lord*** in order to be saved!

No matter who the *"...person..."* may be who preaches that Jesus is Lord, Scripture makes a profoundly important statement about calling Jesus ***Lord***, *"...no one can say that Jesus is Lord except by the Holy Spirit..." (I Corinthians 12:3)*. No matter what a person's IQ may be. No matter what level of education he may have. No matter who his natural family is. No one can know Jesus as ***Lord*** without divine involvement!

We are searching for an answer to the question, *"Why would anyone submit to the rule of Jesus?"*. **The answer is simple:** Anyone who turns his heart toward the Lord desiring to know *"...truth..."* will receive revelation from the Holy Spirit of who Jesus really is! Paul adds understanding to our simple answer in his second letter to the church at Corinth contrasting old covenant ministry with new covenant ministry.

Rewards of Heavenly Submission

> *"For if the ministry of death, written and engraved on stones, was glorious, so that the children of Israel could not look steadily at the face of Moses because of the glory of his countenance, which glory was passing away, how will the ministry of the Spirit not be more glorious? For if the ministry of condemnation had glory, the ministry of righteousness exceeds much more in glory. For even what was made glorious had no glory in this respect, because the glory that excels. For if what is passing away was glorious, what remains is much more glorious. Therefore, since we have such hope, we use great boldness of speech -- unlike Moses, who put a veil over his face so that the children of Israel could not look steadily at the end of what was passing away. But their minds were blinded. For until this day the same veil remains unlifted in the reading of the Old Testament, because the veil is taken away in Christ. But even to this day, when Moses is read, a veil lies on their heart. Nevertheless **when one turns to the Lord, the veil is taken away. Now the Lord is the Spirit; and where the Spirit of the Lord is, there is liberty. But we all, with unveiled face, beholding as in a mirror the glory of the Lord, are being transformed into the same image from glory to glory, just as by the Spirit of the Lord.*" **II Corinthians 3:7-18**

When a person *"...beholds the glory of the Lord..."*, such a person sees Jesus as *"...the way, the truth, and the life. No one comes to the Father except through Me..." (John 14:6)*, and the person sees the truth about his own condition. Seeing Christ as truth and the truth about your own condition from God's perspective are powerful motivators!

In Paul's letter to the church at Ephesus he reminded the Gentile believers...

Submission Defined

*"...remember that you, once Gentiles in the flesh -- who are called Uncircumcision by what is called the Circumcision made in the flesh by hands -- that **at that time you were without Christ, being aliens from the commonwealth of Israel and strangers from the covenants of promise, having no hope and without God in the world.** But now in Christ Jesus you who once were far off have been brought near by the blood of Christ..."* **Ephesians 2:11-13**

To the church at Laodicea Jesus said...

"Because you say, 'I am rich, have become wealthy, and have need of nothing' -- and do not know that you are wretched, miserable, poor, blind, and naked -- I counsel you to buy from Me gold refined in the fire, that you may be rich; and white garments, that you may be clothed, that the shame of your nakedness may not be revealed; and anoint your eyes with eye salve, that you may see..." **Revelation 3:17,18**

When an individual turns his heart toward the Lord, any veil will be taken away *(II Corinthians 3:16)*. The Holy Spirit will provide the individual sight of Jesus as Lord which is the means to be saved from the bondage of his own condition. Such a person will then be able to call Jesus **Lord** *(I Corinthians 12:3)!*

Paul wrote in his second letter to the church at Corinth...

*"...if our gospel is **veiled**, it is **veiled** to those who are perishing, whose minds the god of this age has blinded, who do not believe, lest the light of the gospel of the glory of Christ, who is the image of God, should shine on them..."*
II Corinthians 4:3,4

Rewards of Heavenly Submission

The contrast between a person who has a veil on his heart and a person from whose heart the veil has been removed is monumental! The one who has a veil on his heart *"...**cannot**..."* see the **Lord** because he has a veil on his heart. The one from whose heart the veil has been removed *"...**can**..."* see the **Lord** because the veil has been removed.

According to Scripture, the difference between veiled and unveiled is profoundly simple: The person who turned his heart toward the Lord had his veil removed *(II Corinthians 3:16)*. The person whose veil had not been removed refused to turn his heart toward the Lord and to believe the truth which had been proclaimed to him.

It is true, Paul wrote, *"...if our gospel is **veiled**, it is **veiled** to those who are perishing, **whose minds the god of this age has blinded**, who do not believe..."*. However, *"...the god of this age..."* is not able to *"...blind..."* a person's mind at will. When the gospel is preached...

> *"...not with persuasive words of human wisdom, but in demonstration of the Spirit and of power, that your faith should not be in the wisdom of men but in the power of God." (I Corinthians 2:4,5)...*

...the Holy Spirit provides an anointing for anyone to be able to *"...see..."* so he can believe and be saved!

As already stated, in this dispensation Jesus will not rule by force! A person has freedom to choose to turn his heart toward the Lord and see, to believe or not. His choice will determine whether his heart will be veiled or not.

Submission Defined

If he chooses not to believe, the god of this age will have access to him to blind his mind. Now that is sad! **Veiled** and **blind** are both results of a person's **unwillingness** to believe with his heart turned toward the Lord!

During Jesus' earthly ministry Matthew recorded Jesus often teaching the multitudes in parables. One such parable was the *"...Parable of the Sower..."*. His disciples asked Him why He taught the multitudes in parables. Jesus told them...

> *"...I speak to them in parables, because seeing they do not see, and hearing they do not hear, nor do they understand. And in them the prophecy of Isaiah is fulfilled, which says:*
>
>> *'Hearing you will hear and shall not understand, and seeing you will see and not perceive; **for the hearts of this people have grown dull**. Their ears are hard of hearing, and their eyes they have closed, lest they should see with their eyes and hear with their ears, lest they should understand with their hearts and turn, so that I should heal them.'*
>
> *But blessed are your eyes for they see, and your ears for they hear; for assuredly, I say to you that many prophets and righteous men desired to see what you see, and did not see it, and to hear what you hear, and did not hear it..."*
> **Matthew 13:13-17**

Here Jesus speaks plainly about the multitudes and the condition of their heart using a prophesy prophesied by Isaiah *(Isaiah 6:9,10)* *"...in them the prophecy of Isaiah is fulfilled...**the hearts of this people have grown dull...**"!*

Rewards of Heavenly Submission

Our God *desires* for us to know what He freely reveals!

> *"The secret things belong to the Lord our God, but those things which are revealed belong to us and to our children forever..."* ***Deuteronomy 29:29***

Jesus' interaction with Nicodemus expressed the *desire* of God for *"...the world..."* to be saved...

> *"...For God so loved the world that He gave His only begotten Son, that whoever believes in Him should not perish but have everlasting life. For God did not send His Son into the world to condemn the world, but that the world through Him might be saved."* ***John 3:16,17***

Salvation is available to whomsoever will submit to Jesus as an act of their own free will based on their knowledge of Him *(Romans 10:13-17)*!

Submission opens the door for a person to reap benefit from Jesus as Lord!!!

Chapter Two

From Submission to Un-Submission

The Father raised Jesus from the dead and gave Him the role of ***Lord*** *(Acts 2:32-36)*. This role has great responsibility requiring great authority. Just prior to Jesus' ascension while exhorting and instructing His disciples, He told them *"...all authority has been given to Me in heaven and on earth..." (Matthew 28:18)*. Just think of it, God the Father vested Jesus' role as ***Lord*** with *"...all authority in heaven and on earth..."*.

This understanding has great significance for all who believe. The One whom we call ***Lord*** is the greatest and most powerful of all! Paul wrote of these matters in his letter to the church at Ephesus, asking...

> *"...that the God of our Lord Jesus Christ, the Father of glory, may give to you the spirit of wisdom and revelation in the knowledge of Him, the eyes of your understanding being enlightened; that you may know the hope of His calling, what are the riches of the glory of His inheritance in the saints, and what is the exceeding greatness of His power toward us who believe, according to the working of His mighty power which He worked in Christ when He raised Him from the dead and seated Him at His right hand in the heavenly places, far above all principality and power and might and dominion, and every name that is named, not only in this age but also in that which is to come. And He put all things under His feet, and gave Him to be head over all things to the church, which is His body, the fullness of Him who fills all in all." **Ephesians 1:20-23***

Rewards of Heavenly Submission

For the body of Christ, submission to Jesus as ***Lord*** is designed to be a way of life, not merely the means of being born again! Jesus as head over *"...all things to the church, which is His body..."* requires the submission of every part of His body. ***We reap benefit from Jesus as Lord and from His authority by "...submitting..." to Him!***

In his letter to *"...brethren..."* from *"...the twelve tribes which are scattered abroad..." (**James 1:1,2**)*, James addressed believers' foolish choice of moving from submission to unsubmission. His inspired use of terms were *severe*.

> *"Come now, you who say, 'Today or tomorrow we will go to such and such a city, spend a year there, buy and sell, and make a profit'; whereas you do not know what will happen tomorrow, for what is your life? It is even a vapor that appears for a little time and then vanishes away. Instead you ought to say, 'If the Lord wills, we shall live and do this or that.' **But now you boast in your arrogance. All such boasting is evil.** Therefore, to him who knows to do good and does not do it, to him it is sin." **James 4:13-17***

These *"...brethren..."* had submitted to Jesus as ***Lord*** at some point in their lives in order to be called *"...brethren..."*. The severity of James' rebuke revolved around the believers' mind-set of submission illustrated by their statements, *'...Today or tomorrow we will go to such and such a city, spend a year there, buy and sell, and make a profit." (**James 4:13**)*. The stringent terminology the Holy Spirit inspired James to use referring to these statements is frightening; *"...now you boast in your arrogance. All such boasting is evil..." (**James 4:16**)*.

From Submission to Un-Submission

James wrote why God views Jesus' role as **Lord** concerning the future so important!

> "...you do not know what will happen tomorrow, for what is your life? It is even a vapor that appears for a little time and then vanishes away..."

No believer can know the future in his own power, but Jesus the **Lord** with "...all authority in heaven and on earth..." does. To make decisions that will affect your future in the power of your own might without input from the **Lord** would be carnal, uncertain, and foolish. Surely, no one would do such a thing unless he had been deceived.

To add to this understanding we look again at what has already been stated.

> "The revelation of Jesus as **Lord** is the cornerstone around which the entire church is built *(I Peter 2:1-10)*! Salvation itself is predicated on the **Lordship** of Christ! In other words, God has chosen Jesus as **Lord** to be the doorway through which a person must pass to be saved!"

> "For the body of Christ, submission to Jesus as **Lord** is designed to be a way of life, not merely the means of being born again!"

Acts of un-submission by any believer who previously *submitted* to the **Lord** is equivalent to that believer saying he does not need Jesus as **Lord** by which to live! That would help explain why the Holy Spirit inspired James to write as he did regarding business decisions made without input from the **Lord**.

Rewards of Heavenly Submission

Jesus Himself addressed such a condition in the lives of the church at Laodicea.

> "...Because you say, 'I am rich, have become wealthy, and have need of nothing'-- and do not know that you are wretched, miserable, poor, blind, and naked -- I counsel you to buy from Me gold refined in the fire, that you may be rich; and white garments, that you may be clothed, that the shame of your nakedness may not be revealed; and anoint your eyes with eye salve, that you may see..." **Revelation 3:17,18**

Our **unwillingness** to submit as a way of life testifies we believe we do not need Jesus as **Lord** to live our daily lives! No matter how mature we may grow in our knowledge of the **Lord**, no matter how great our faith may become, no matter what role we may fulfill in His church, we will never reach a level we do not need Jesus as **Lord** as the means by which to live our daily lives! He is *"...the way, the truth, the life..." (John 14:6)*!

Submission to Jesus as Lord
is designed to be a way of life,
not merely the means of being born again!

Revelation freely given to us by God says, *"...by grace you have been saved through faith, and that not of yourselves; it is the gift of God..." (Ephesians 2:8)*, and *"...No one can say that Jesus is Lord except by the Holy Spirit..." (I Corinthians 12:3)*. The old covenant was made *"...obsolete..." (Hebrews 8:13)* because it was based on man's ability to do the will of God. The new covenant is designed to be done by persons with abilities provided by God! Man's ability to say

From Submission to Un-Submission

Jesus is **Lord** and man's ability to live in Christ can only be done with divine enablement! This is the fundamental difference between the old covenant and the new covenant: *man's ability versus divine ability.*

It is the ability given to us by the Holy Spirit which enables us to see and call Jesus Lord. It is the ability given to us by Abba whereby we accept Jesus to be saved. At the time of our new birth we were made new creatures in Christ, given a new heart, and ordained to walk as spiritual rather than natural, mere men. The enemy is constantly endeavoring to steal, kill, and destroy any hope we have of living as spiritual men. His devices are subtle and crafty designed to deceive. We must awaken to truth and escape from the power of the enemy's devices!

Paul was constantly *"...stewarding..."* the mysteries he preached and the believers' response to them *(I Corinthians 4:1)*. His desire was for the word to produce life in the people. As a steward Paul rebuked the church at Corinth for walking as carnal, mere men instead of spiritual people *(I Corinthians 3:1-23)*. In his second letter to this troubled church, Paul wrote *"...we walk by faith, not by sight..." (II Corinthians 5:7)*. Paul wrote to the church at Galatia, *"O foolish Galatians! Who has bewitched you...Are you so foolish? Having begun in the spirit, are you now being made perfect by the flesh..." (Galatians 3:1,3)*. In this same letter to the Galatians, Paul wrote, *"...Walk in the spirit and you shall not fulfill the lust of the flesh..." **(Galatians 5:16)**.*

Rewards of Heavenly Submission

Walking by faith as a spiritual new creature is an act of submission each believer must make based on the knowledge he has of the will of Jesus the **Lord!** Paul's ministry to these believers in Corinth, Galatia, and ultimately to us, is ordained to awaken us to the will of God regarding the Lord's design for the church! Submission is not required as a means of control but so that we may partake of the benefits of Jesus' role as **Lord!**

After seeing Jesus as Lord and our own human condition by the power provided by the Holy Spirit, ***how does a person shift from submission to unsubmission?*** Finding an answer to this question is pivotal in helping us avoid making such a shift. The answer is intimately linked to temptation.

> *"Let no one say when he is tempted, 'I am tempted by God'; for God cannot be tempted by evil, nor does He Himself tempt anyone. But each one is tempted when he is drawn away by his own desires and enticed. Then when desire has conceived, it gives birth to sin; and sin, when it is full-grown, brings forth death..."* ***James 1:13-15***

At the time of our new birth we are made new creatures in Christ! This new creature condition is directly related to our spirit, not our flesh. After being born again our flesh is not changed, only our spirit. Every born again new creature in Christ is both a natural creature and a spiritual creature. Everyone born again must attend to the desires of his natural flesh and the desires of his spirit. All natural desires of the flesh are not in violation of the will of God. Paul provides understanding of when and how fleshly desires are in violation of the will of God.

From Submission to Un-Submission

Paul wrote extensively about the subject of the flesh in relation to the human spirit and the Holy Spirit. To the church at Rome he wrote:

> "...those who live according to the flesh set their minds on the things of the flesh, but those who live according to the Spirit, the things of the Spirit For to be carnally (4561) minded is death, but to be spiritually minded is life and peace. Because the carnal mind is enmity against God; for it is not subject to the law of God, nor indeed can be..."
> **Romans 8:5-7 NKJV**

> "...they that are after the flesh do mind the things of the flesh; but they that are after the Spirit the things of the Spirit. For to be carnally minded is death: but to be spiritually minded is life and peace. Because the carnal mind is enmity against God: for it is not subject to the law of God, neither indeed can be..." **Romans 8:5-7 KJV**

Verse 5 in the *NKJV* says, "...those who live according to the flesh...". The same verse in the *KJV* says, "...those who are after the flesh...". Although subtle perhaps, the difference between these two versions is stark. Without building "...doctrine..." around different versions of the Bible, it is better to look a little deeper into the context from which *Verse 5* is taken. Immediately following this verse but still considering the same subject, Paul says to be "...carnally (4561) minded is death...". Having natural desires of the flesh is not a violation of the will of God, being carnally minded is!

> *What is carnally minded?*

4561 sarx prob. from the base of *4663*; *flesh* (as *stripped away from the skin*), i. e. (strictly) the *meat* of an animal (as food), or (by extens.) the *body* (as opposed to the soul [or spirit], or as the symbol of what is external, or as the means of kindred), or (by impl.) *human nature* (with its frailties [phys. or mor.] and passions), or (spec.) a *human being* (as such): carnal (-ly, + -ly minded), flesh ([-ly]).

<u>**Strong's Exhaustive Concordance of the Bible**</u>

Carnally minded is simply a person having their priorities in life oriented to the outer natural man, rather than the inner spiritual man. The priority of a person's life determines whether a person lives after the flesh or after the spirit. If a person's priority is the external natural fleshly part of his existence, *he will be carnally minded.* If a person's priority is the internal spiritual part of his existence, *he will be spiritually minded.* **The priority of our lives determines the quality and destiny of our lives!**

Jesus is the best possible illustration of a person having a spiritual priority and the reward for such a choice. Jesus partook of *"...flesh and blood..."* **(Hebrews 2:14)** *"...in that He Himself has suffered, being tempted, He is able to aid those who are tempted..."* **(Hebrews 2:18)**. Jesus was tempted! It would be of great benefit to consider Jesus' temptation in the wilderness.

> *"Then Jesus, being filled with the Holy Spirit, returned from the Jordan and was led by the Spirit into the wilderness, being tempted for forty days by the devil. And in those days He ate nothing, and afterward, when they had ended, He was hungry (3983). And the devil said to Him, 'If You are the Son of God, command this stone to become bread.' But Jesus answered him, saying, 'It is written, 'Man shall not live by bread alone, but by every word of God.'..."* **Luke 4:1-4**

From Submission to Un-Submission

Verse 2 says *"...being tempted for forty days by the devil. And in those days He ate nothing, and afterward, when they had ended, He was hungry (3983)...".*

> *3983 pelnao* from the same as *3993* (through the idea of pinching *toil; "pine"*); to *famish* (absol. or comparatively); fig. to *crave:* -- *be an hungered.*

The devil said to Jesus in the wilderness, *'...If You are the Son of God, command this stone to become bread....'*. In order for this to be considered a real *"...temptation..."*, Jesus' flesh had to have desired food. According to **Strong's** definition of the Greek term *pelnao* used to describe Jesus' condition, Jesus was not just hungry, He was famished. His flesh craved food.

Yet, according to James' writing, the *"...desire..."* of Jesus' flesh for food was not sin simply because his flesh desired it, *"...each one is tempted when he is drawn away by his own desires and enticed. Then when desire has conceived, it gives birth to sin..."* **(James 1:13-15)**. **Desire** alone is not sin; it must conceive to give birth to sin. In order for the desire of the flesh to conceive, such desires must be the *priority* of a person's life. The *priority* of Jesus' life was not His outer natural flesh. This would have made Him carnally minded. Jesus' *priority* was spiritual and all things God. This made Him spiritually minded.

As a spiritually minded man He saw the desires of His flesh simply as natural hunger. Even though Jesus understood the starving condition of His flesh, He processed the desires of His flesh as a spiritual minded man and said to the devil, *"...It is written, 'Man shall not live by bread alone, but by every word of God.'..."* **(Luke 4:4)**.

Rewards of Heavenly Submission

Jesus was submitted to do only the will of His Father *(John 5:30)*. Jesus placed such a high value on Scripture that He demonstrated His submission by quoting what He knew to be *"... written..."* as the will of God! Jesus desired the things of the spirit more than the things of the flesh. Jesus was a spiritually minded man fully submitted to God and the Word of God!

We are searching for an answer to the question, *"How does a person shift from submission to unsubmission?"*. The moment a believer shifts from submission to unsubmission he places himself in grave danger of being taken captive by the enemy. Finding an answer for how to avoid making this shift is pivotal in helping us avoid being taken captive.

The first step of the shift comes with temptation to yield to the desires of the flesh: *"...Each one is tempted when he is drawn away by his own desires and enticed. Then when desire has conceived, it gives birth to sin..."* **James 1:13,14**. Make no mistake about it, every person's flesh is going to have desires. Jesus' flesh did! Yet, He did not sin because He was spiritually minded.

If the priority of our lives is the outer natural flesh, we will be carnally minded: *"...to be carnally minded is death, but to be spiritually minded is life and peace. Because the carnal mind is enmity against God; for it is not subject to the law of God, nor indeed can be..."* **(Romans 8:6,7)**. If we are carnally minded when we are tempted by the desire of our own flesh, conception will take place, we will yield to the desire of our flesh, and that will give birth to sin. Because *"...the carnal mind is enmity against God..."*, **a carnally minded person cannot be submitted to God!**

From Submission to Un-Submission

A person is only able to see and to call Jesus Lord by the Holy Spirit *(I Corinthians 12:3)*. Even if a person has submitted to the will and ability of God to both see and to call Jesus Lord, he can at any time choose to make the desires of his flesh his *priority*. The believers to whom James wrote *(James 4:13-17)* and the church at Laodicea to whom Jesus spoke *(Revelation 3:14-22)* are two examples of believers making the desires of their flesh their priority.

The moment a believer chooses to make the desires of his flesh his priority he shifts from submission to unsubmission. The person does not become unsaved, just unsubmitted. This unsubmission closes the door on Jesus as a way of life, just as it did in the lives of the believers to whom James wrote and the Laodiceans! Jesus said to the Laodiceans...

> "...Behold, I stand at the door and knock. If anyone hears My voice and opens the door, I will come in to him and dine with him, and he with Me..." **Revelation 3:20**

It is important to note here that a carnally minded person is a person who has chosen to make the desires of his flesh the *priority* of his life. It is easy to assess whether the desires of our flesh are the *priority* of our life or the things of the spirit are our *priority!* Beware, the enemy has pulled out all the stops in an effort to steal any hope the church may have of living as spiritually minded people! Nevertheless, God's standard to distinguish the difference between carnally minded and spiritually minded is simple: *Follow the standard of God.*

Rewards of Heavenly Submission

"For I say, through the grace given to me, to everyone who is among you, not to think of himself more highly than he ought to think, but to think soberly, as God has dealt to each one a measure of faith..." **Romans 12:3**

➤ ***Carnally minded*** is the result of a person making the things of his outer natural flesh the priority of his life.

➤ ***Spiritually minded*** is the result of a person making the things of the spirit *(and the kingdom of God)* the priority of his life.

> *The only way to be submitted to God is to be spiritually minded!*

Chapter Three

Submission Between Believers

"Awake, you who sleep, arise from the dead, and Christ will give you light. See then that you walk circumspectly, not as fools but as wise, redeeming the time, because the days are evil. Therefore do not be unwise, but understand what the will of the Lord is. And do not be drunk with wine, in which is dissipation; but be filled with the Spirit, speaking to one another in psalms and hymns and spiritual songs, singing and making melody in your heart to the Lord, giving thanks always for all things to God the Father in the name of our Lord Jesus Christ, **submitting (5293 hupotasso) to one another in the fear of God.***"* **Ephesians 5:15-21**

The same Greek term *"...hupotasso..."* and the English term *"...submit..."* considered in *Chapter One* in relation to a person submitting to the rule of Christ are also used in reference to *"...submission between believers...".* In order to provide a simple definition of *"...submission...",* we applied **Strong's** definition of *"...submit..." (Chapter One, page 3).* And since there is no *"...rod of iron..."* in Jesus' rule in this dispensation, we stated, *"...submission is simply a person's willingness to yield to the rule of Christ...".* **How does this understanding apply to submission between believers?** *Fundamentally the same!*

Submission between believers is a willingness to yield *"...bound..."* to the revelation of *"...agreement...".* The wisdom of God spoken through Amos the prophet expressed the concept of agreement in the form of a rhetorical question: *"Can two walk together, except they be agreed?" (Amos 3:3).* In order for members of Christ's body to walk together, they must be agreed. This type of agreement is God centered, not man based. Members of Christ's body successfully walking together from God's perspective are not merely two persons coming into agreement with the will of one another.

A believer was involved in sexually immoral acts in the church at Corinth with his father's wife.

> *"It is actually reported that there is sexual immorality among you, and such sexual immorality as is not even named among the Gentiles -- that a man has his father's wife. And you are puffed up, and have not rather mourned, that he who has done this deed might be taken away from among you. For I indeed, as absent in body but present in spirit, have already judged (as though I were present) him who has so done this deed."* **I Corinthians 5:1-3**

The woman involved in this sexual immorality may also have been a believer, but Paul only makes reference to *"...he who has done this deed..."* and *"...I...have already judged **him**..."*.

There is no Scriptural reference to this man *"...forcing..."* his father's wife into this sexual immorality. Rather, the implication is they were both in agreement to commit this or these acts. This type of agreement does not conform to God's will and is certainly not the expression of agreement needed between believers in the church today. Even though these two persons were walking together in agreement, God was not involved in nor pleased with their actions.

Submission Between Believers

Agreement between believers walking together must be in accordance with the will of God! Two believers as believers can only successfully walk together in agreement with one another according to the measure each is in agreement with God. Man's agreement with man must be Christ centered in order for believers to walk together successfully in the church.

A believer merely giving mental assent to the will of the Lord is not walking in agreement with the Lord. Agreement from God's perspective is a believer agreeing with what he knows is the will of the Lord and being a *"...doer..."* of that will. Any believer in agreement with Christ will be submitted to the rule of Christ.

Successfully walking together as believers in the church requires knowledge of the will of the Lord regarding His design for the church on the earth. If believers desire to walk together on the earth as functional parts of the church, they must do so in agreement with what each knows to be the will of the Lord.

> *A believer's submission to the rule of Christ is foundational for "...submission between believers..."!*

Every time two believers come into agreement with one another according to the will of the Lord, they are re-affirming their submission to the rule of the Lord!

Rewards of Heavenly Submission

The enemy has a subtle but extremely destructive device he uses against the church in an effort to corrupt the individual believer's submission to the rule of Christ! This de-vice is so destructive because it attempts to change the stan-dard whereby we measure our lives. The device endeavors to make a minister, other believers, or other churches the standard by which a believer measures his own life instead of Christ as the standard. **Christ must always be our standard!**

Here is one of the primary ways this device works. A minister presents a certain revelation designed to be a part of the daily operation of the church. The revelation is clearly able to be seen in Scripture and confirmed by the anointing. However, the minister may not have successfully walked out this revelation in his own life although he knows he must be a doer. The revelation may be in the process of being restored in the church and not operational in the lives of believers and churches yet. Nevertheless, the revelation is still the will of the Lord and needed in the church.

The enemy seeks a willing vessel. This will typically be a believer who is unwilling to do what the Lord is revealing in the revelation the minister has presented. Such a believer's resistance is most often ***indirect***, not pure rebellion against the Lord! This indirect resistance has a language all its own. The *"...resistant-unwilling-believer..."* speaks to the minister who presented the revelation: *"This revelation is not operational in your life, the lives of other believers, nor in other churches. Therefore, you cannot ask me to do it!"*

Submission Between Believers

It is absolutely essential for every minister who freely gives any revelation he has freely received to be a doer himself! And all believers are to be *"...doers..."* of the word they receive. However, lack of skill in a minister being a *"...doer..."* or lack of other believers being *"...doers..."* do not qualify as *"...**excuses**..."* for a believer to refuse to do the will of the Lord! Jesus is our standard, not ministers, other believers, nor a void of any aspect of the Lord's will in the church!

The *"...will of the Lord..."* is not determined by any minister's skill level in the Word or other believers level of submission to the will of the Lord. These things simply must not serve as excuses to invalidate the word of the Lord as the will of the Lord in the life of any believer. ***No minister or believer or church is ever to become the standard for our lives! Christ is always our standard!*** The enemy has many devices with which he tempts men to change the standard of Christ, ***however, new covenant faith is designed to always be in Christ, not men!***

Apostles, prophets, evangelists, pastors, and teachers have been given by Christ *"...till we all come to the unity of the faith and of the knowledge of the Son of God, to a perfect man, to the measure of the stature of the fullness of Christ..."* **(Ephesians 4:13)**. The enemy hates this foundational truth and devotes an enormous amount of time and energy trying to corrupt it. The enemy's desire is for believers to use anything, but especially *"...ministers through whom you believed..."* **(I Corinthians 3:5)**, as a substitute for Christ in one form or another. If believers follow ministers as a substitute for Christ in any way, the enemy will surely rule the church.

Rewards of Heavenly Submission

How does the enemy seem to so easily install this device in the church?

The answer is simple:

If a believer submits to a minister as a minister prior to submitting to that minister as a believer, error will follow!

All submission within the church must begin with each individual believers' submission to Jesus as Lord! The next step of submission must be believer to believer, not believer to minister! All relationships in the church are to be founded on life as believers, first believer to Christ, then believer to believer, and only then believer to minister.

The writer of the letter to the Hebrews wrote,

> *"Remember those who rule over you, who have spoken the word of God to you, whose faith follow, considering the outcome of their conduct."* **Hebrews 13:7**

Even though words *"...who rule over you..."* are used, the context of the words provide instructions *"...whose faith follow...".* We are to follow the *"...faith..."* of those who rule over us as their *"...faith is in Christ Jesus...".*

Christ is always to have the preeminence!

Submission Between Believers

Submission is *not* the will of the Lord in order for Jesus nor the ministers whom He has placed in the church to gain *"...control..."* over us. Submission opens the door for us to be able to reap benefit from Jesus' role as **Lord!** If *"...submission between believers..."* works correctly, it, too, will open a door to the supernatural power of God. Jesus told His disciples...

> *"...He who receives you receives Me, and he who receives Me receives Him who sent Me..."* **Matthew 10:40**

Jesus is *"...the way, the truth, and the life..." (John 14:6)*. Only accurate knowledge of the truth will lead us to Christ! John contrasted *"...the spirit of truth and the spirit of error..."* in his first epistle.

> "Beloved, do not believe every spirit, but test the spirits, whether they are of God; because many false prophets have gone out into the world. By this you know the Spirit of God: Every spirit that confesses that Jesus Christ has come in the flesh is of God, and every spirit that does not confess that Jesus Christ has come in the flesh is not of God. And this is the spirit of the Antichrist, which you have heard was coming, and is now already in the world. You are of God, little children, and have overcome them, because He who is in you is greater than he who is in the world. They are of the world. Therefore they speak as of the world, and the world hears them. We are of God. He who knows God hears us; he who is not of God does not hear us. By this we know the spirit of truth and the spirit of error." *I John 5:1-6*

My wife and I were members of ***Wycliffe Bible Translators***. We spent four years in Papua New Guinea as translation personnel living in a remote village in the mangrove swamps just

Rewards of Heavenly Submission

off of the coast of the Bismarck Sea. In this setting the Lord Jesus required me to assess everything I "...believed...".

This assessment was to determine what I believed, why I believed it, and if it was working as the way I lived. The assessment revealed I did not have any doctrines based on error. However, I did believe some things I had been taught by others that I had not affirmed by the Word and which were not working in my life. No matter who teaches you, it must be affirmed by the Word, confirmed by the Holy Spirit, and become a way of life as you become *"...doers of the word, and not hearers only, deceiving yourselves..." **(James 1:22)**.*

The lives of the members of the church can only be successful in Christ if they are based on accurate knowledge of the truth which leads them to Christ! Submission to the Lord must be based on accurate knowledge of Him. Any attempt to submit to Jesus as Lord based on tradition, the doc-trine of men, or doctrine which has not been affirmed by the Word and confirmed by the Holy Spirit will not produce a viable personal relationship between the believer and Jesus.

Perhaps the most dramatic illustration of this understanding is revealed by Jesus speaking to people who called Him *"... Lord, Lord..."* believing they were submitted to Him as Lord...

> *"...Not everyone who says to Me, 'Lord, Lord.' shall enter the kingdom of heaven, but he who does the will of My Father in heaven. Many will say to Me in that day, 'Lord, Lord, have we not prophesied in Your name, cast out demons in Your*

Submission Between Believers

name, and done many wonders in Your name?' And then I will declare to them, 'I never knew you; depart from Me, you who practice lawlessness!" **Matthew 7:21-23**

Clearly these people believed they were submitted to the Lord because Jesus said, *"...Many will say to Me in that day, 'Lord, Lord'..."*. It is also equally clear these same people calling Jesus *"...'Lord, Lord'..."* did not have a viable personal relationship with Him because Jesus said, *"...then I will declare to them, 'I never knew you...'*. ***Tragic!***

A viable personal relationship with Jesus is only possible through accurate knowledge of Him. He will only accept a person's submission to Him based on accurate knowledge of the truth. If a person's knowledge of the truth is not accurate, any attempt to submit to Jesus based on these inaccuracies will not produce a viable personal relationship with Jesus. Any submission a believer gives to a fellow believer or to a minister based on inaccurate knowledge of the truth will lead to error!

Rewards of Heavenly Submission

Chapter Four

Jesus' Submission to His Father

"In the beginning was the Word, and the Word was with God, and the Word was God. He was in the beginning with God. All things were made through Him, and without Him nothing was made that was made. In Him was life, and the life was the light of men. And the light shines in the darkness, and the darkness did not comprehend it. There was a man sent from God, whose name was John. This man came for a witness, to bear witness of the Light, that all through him might believe. He was not that Light, but was sent to bear witness of that Light. That was the true Light which gives light to every man coming into the world. He was in the world, and the world was made through Him, and the world did not know Him. He came to His own, and His own did not receive Him. But as many as received Him, to them He gave the right to become children of God, to those who believe in His name who were born, not of blood, nor of the will of the flesh, nor of the will of man, but of God. And the Word became flesh and dwelt among us, and we beheld His glory, the glory as of the only begotten of the Father, full of grace and truth. John bore witness of Him and cried out, saying, 'This was He of whom I said, He who comes after me is preferred before me, for He was before me.' And of His fullness we have all received, and grace for grace. For the law was given through Moses, but grace and truth came through Jesus Christ. No one has seen God at any time. The only begotten Son, who is in the bosom of the Father, He has declared Him." **John 1:1-18**

Rewards of Heavenly Submission

The **Word of God**, who was in the beginning *"...with God, and the Word was God..."*, transitioned into *"...the man Jesus..."*. This transition took place through the *"...virgin Mary's..."* conception and subsequent delivery of the baby Jesus. Although Jesus *"...**did not stop being God**..."*, it was His *choice* as God to divest Himself of His divine attributes, be made *"...flesh and blood..."*, and live on earth as a *"...**man**..."*.

> *"Inasmuch then as the children have partaken of flesh and blood, He Himself likewise shared in the same, that through death He might destroy him who had the power of death, that is, the devil."* **Hebrews 2:14**

> *"...Sacrifice and offering You did not desire, but **a body You have prepared for Me**. In burnt offerings and sacrifices for sin You had no pleasure. Then I said, 'Behold, I have come -- in the volume of the book it is written of Me -- to do Your will, O God.' ...By that will we have been sanctified **through the offering of the body of Jesus Christ** once for all."* **Hebrews 10:1-10**

God made man *"...in His own image..." (**Genesis 1:27**)*. Man is comprised of three parts: *spirit, soul, and body*. These three parts are unique to each person, like fingerprints or DNA. Every person's existence is established by their own unique three parts. God is comprised of three unique parts, as is man, because man is made *"...in God's own image..."*. No one part of God is any less or any more God than the other two parts. All three parts of the Trinity are equally God. However, when **God the Word** chose to divest Himself of His divine attributes in order to partake of *"...flesh and blood..."*, He *chose* not to live on the earth as God, but as man. With this *choice* He changed the basis of how He would relate to the other two parts of the Trinity.

Jesus' Submission to His Father

When the ***Word of God*** *"...became flesh..."*, He partook of the DNA of Mary. Being willing to be birthed into this world as Mary's *"...flesh and blood..."* son was an act of His will as ***God the Word***. Because the *"...flesh and blood..."* Jesus' mother Mary was a virgin, her miraculous conception was only possible by the power of God! Mary's immaculate conception accomplished by the power of God made Jesus *"...the only begotten Son..."* of God!

In the *fifth chapter of the Gospel According to John* Jesus repeatedly spoke of being *"...sent by God His Father..."* and that He did not fulfill His ministry in His own abilities.

> *"I can of Myself do nothing. As I hear, I judge; and My judgment is righteous, because I do not seek My own will but the will of **the Father who sent Me**."* **John 5:30**
> *(See context **John 5:19-47**; esp. 19-23; 26,27; 43)*

Just prior to His earthly departure, John recorded Jesus telling His disciples He was *"...going to the Father..."*, and, then, He made a most remarkable comparison between Himself and His Father,

> *"You have heard Me say to you, 'I am going away and coming back to you.' If you loved Me, you would rejoice because I said, 'I am going to the Father,' for..."*

> **"My Father is greater than I!"**
> ***John 14:28***

Rewards of Heavenly Submission

Paul wrote a wonderful synopsis of the transition of the *"...Word as God..."* to *"...Jesus as man..."* and the effects of this transition in the letter to the saints which are in Philippi.

> *"Let this mind be in you which was also in Christ Jesus, who, being in the form of God, did not consider it robbery to be equal with God, but made Himself of no repu-tation, taking the form of a bond-servant, He humbled Himself and became obedient to the point of death, even the death of the cross. Therefore God also has highly exalted Him and given Him the name which is above every name, that at the name of Jesus every knee should bow, of those in heaven, and of those on earth, and of those under the earth, and that every tongue should confess that Jesus Christ is Lord, to the glory of God the Father."* **Philippians 2:5-11**

Certainly, *as God*, it was within His prerogative to divest Himself of His divine attributes, to become *"...flesh and blood..."*, and to live on earth as **the man Jesus!** The other two parts of the Trinity did not *"...force..."* **God the Word** to become *"...flesh and blood..."*. **God the Word** *"...submitted..."* to this incredible plan!

Embedded in Jesus' conversation with Nicodemus, the powerful motive by which the Triune God conceived this plan is revealed: "...*love...*"!

> *"**For God so loved the world** that He gave His only begotten Son, that whoever believes in Him should not perish but have everlasting life. For God did not send His Son into the world to condemn the world, but that the world through Him might be saved."* **John 3:16,17**

Jesus' Submission to His Father

Contained in verse sixteen is a subtle but deeply profound revelation! John wrote it was *"...God.."* who *"... loved the world..."*. Because God is a Triune God, then all three parts of the Trinity loved the world. **God the Word** *"...so loved the world..."* that He was willing to partake of *"...flesh and blood..."* to become *"...the only begotten Son of God..."* in order to redeem man from the power of darkness and to be made Lord of a kingdom in which the redeemed could live *(Colossians 1:13)*.

In *John 3:16,17* Jesus was speaking to Nicodemus as *"...the only begotten Son of God..."*. However, speaking as *"...the only begotten Son of God..."* was His choice. Scripture is clear that Jesus *"...being in the form of God, did not consider it robbery to be equal with God, but made Himself of no reputation, taking the form of a bond-servant, He humbled Himself and became obedient to the point of death, even the death of the cross..."* *(Philippians 2:5-8)*. The words *"...made Himself of no reputation, taking the form of a bond-servant, He humbled Himself..."* are terms of **submission**, not subjugation.

Everything **God the Word** did after He became **Jesus the man** demonstrated tender submission to His Father and great love for us. As has already been stated *(see page 34)*:

> "...when **God the Word** *chose* to divest Himself of His divine attributes in order to partake of flesh and blood, He *chose* not to live on the earth as God, but as man. With this *choice* He changed the basis of how He would relate to the other two parts of the Trinity...."

Jesus' reference to God as His Father revealed the *choice* He made as **God the Word** to submit to the plan of salvation, to partake of *"...flesh and blood..."*, and to become *"...the only begotten Son of God..."*.

Rewards of Heavenly Submission

As inconceivable as it may be, the transition of the Word of God into the man Jesus was a process. Although this process began with a miraculous supernatural event, the instant the **Word of God** entered this world, impregnating the Virgin Mary, Jesus' life began as a *human*. This was **God the Word's choice**: to divest Himself of His divine attributes, to partake of *"...flesh and blood..."*, to live on earth as a *man*. Immediately following the immaculate conception, the **Word of God** became *"...flesh and blood..."* through the normal human process of a woman's full-term pregnancy and normal human birthing. Laying in the manger, wrapped in swaddling clothes, newly birthed into this world was **God the Word** *"...clothed in flesh..."* come to dwell among us as Jesus, *"...the only begotten Son of God...".*

Was this Jesus God? Yes, He absolutely was God! However, as God He had the Sovereign right and ability to lay aside His divine attributes and to come into this world as *"...flesh and blood..."*. That is exactly what He did! In order for **God the Word** to *"...partake of flesh and blood..." (Hebrews 2:14)*, He *chose* to be birthed into the world as an infant and grow through all the stages of life as any other flesh and blood child. One thing must remain alive in our understanding:

> *Jesus "...chose..." to live as a man even though He was God!*

Entering this world as *"...flesh and blood..."* initiated the plan of salvation with which **God the Word** was fully agreed. As one part of the Trinity, **God the Word** knew that when He divested

Jesus' Submission to His Father

Himself of His divine attributes, He would not function as God during His earthly ministry but as *"...the only begotten Son of God...".* **God the Word's agreement** with the other two parts of the Trinity regarding this plan transitioned into the man Jesus' *submission* to His Father *(See **Philippians 2:5-11**).*

God the Word clothed in flesh became the little boy Jesus! As a little boy Jesus participated in the laws and customs of His family. Because He was Birthed into a Jewish family, Jewish law required Him to be circumcised *(**Luke 2:21**)*. As a little boy Jesus had to *"...grow..." physically, mentally, and spiritually* in order to reach maturity as the man Jesus.

> *"And the Child grew and became strong in spirit, filled with wisdom; and the grace of God was upon Him."* **Luke 2:40**

John recorded Jesus declaring some remarkable things about Himself as the *"...Son of God...".*

> *"Most assuredly, I say to you, the Son can do nothing of Himself, but what He sees the Father do; for whatever He does, the Son also does in like manner."* **John 5:19**

> *"I can of Myself do nothing. As I hear, I judge; and My judgment is righteous, because I do not seek My own will but the will of the Father who sent Me."* **John 5:30**

It was Jesus' willingness to do the will of His Father which released the Father's will to be made known to Him *(Compare **John 7:16-18** about "...how to know the will of God...".)*. Jesus as *"...the only begotten Son of God..."* was submitted to His Father's will even to the point of death.

Rewards of Heavenly Submission

> *"...He (Jesus) humbled Himself and became obedient to the point of death, even the death of the cross..."*
> **Philippians 2:8**

We established a simple definition for *"...submission..."* within the church regarding men's relationship with the Lord in **Chapter One, page three** as *"...a person's willingness to yield to the rule of Christ...".* If we apply this definition to the man Jesus' relationship with God His Father, it would read, *"...Jesus' willingness to yield to the rule of His Father...".*

Just imagine, **God the Word** *chose* to divest Himself of His divine attributes and to come to the earth to live as the man Jesus because of His love for us! He did not walk on the earth as God nor fulfill His ministry in His own power as God. **God the Word** walked on the earth as **Jesus the man** and fulfilled His ministry in *submission* to the will and power of God His Father and God the Holy Spirit! **What kind of love was this?!**

Consider the link between Jesus' humble submission to His Father and His Father's *"...highly exalting Him...".*

> *"...Christ Jesus, who, being in the form of God, did not consider it robbery to be equal with God, but made Himself of no reputation, taking the form of a bond-servant, He humbled Himself and became obedient to the point of death, even the death of the cross.* **Therefore** *God also has highly exalted Him and given Him the name which is above every name..."* **Philippians 2:5-11**

Jesus *"...humbled Himself and became obedient...Therefore God also has highly exalted Him..."!* The link between humble submission and God exalting such a person is a revelation seen through the

Jesus' Submission to His Father

entire Bible. This revelation can be seen in the New Testament in Peter's epistle, *I Peter 5:5-11*, using almost identical words found in *Philippians 2:8,9*.

> 'God resists the proud, but gives grace to the humble.'
>
> "Therefore humble yourselves under the mighty hand of God, that He may exalt you in due time..." *I Peter 5:5,6*

Philippians 2:5-11 considering Jesus' life in relation to God His Father begins with *"Let this mind be in you which was also in Christ Jesus..."*. John wrote in his first epistle, *"He who says he abides in Him ought himself also to walk just as He walked." I John 2:6.*
With Jesus as our pattern, we, too, are to...

"*...humble ourselves and become obedient...*"
to the Lord! He will "*...exalt us in due time...*"!

Rewards of Heavenly Submission

Chapter Five

Diversity of Submission

By definition *"...submission is a willingness to yield to the rule or authority of another..."*. There is a vertical component in this definition. The person willingly yielding to another will necessarily place himself *"...under..."* the person to whom he is yielding. A really important note must be made here restating the contrast between submission and subjugation. Submission is a willingness to yield to the rule of another. Subjugation is being ruled by force. Subjugation in the church is anti-Christ!

A person enters the kingdom as a babe-in-Christ. Just as babes in the natural world, spiritual babes must be overseen with constant care. A babe-in-Christ must willingly place himself under the care of another believer to make his submission holy. The only way any believer will see correctly in order to willingly place himself under the care of another is to be spiritually minded. According to Scripture a spiritually minded person *"...lives according to the things of the spirit..."* **NKJV** or *"...is after the things of the spirit..."* **KJV (Romans 8:4)**.

As a babe-in-Christ grows in his knowledge of the Word and in his skill in the use of the Word, God expects him to freely give to others what he has freely received. The writer of the letter to the Hebrews specifically addressed this expectation.

Rewards of Heavenly Submission

> *"For though by this time you ought to be teachers, you need someone to teach you again the first principles of the oracles of God; and you have come to need milk and not solid food. For everyone who partakes only of milk is unskilled in the word of righteousness, for he is a babe. But solid food belongs to those who are of full age, that is, those who by reason of use have their senses exercised to discern both good and evil. Therefore, leaving the discussion of the elementary principles of Christ, let us go on to perfection, not laying again the foundation of repentance from dead works and of faith toward God, of the doctrine of baptisms, of laying on of hands, of resurrection of the dead, and of eternal judgment. And this we will do if God permits."*
>   **Hebrews 5:12-6:3**

There is no indication this letter was written to those called to the vocational ministry of *"..teacher..."*. The content of the letter is written to believers. **Chapter three verse one** directly refers to the readers as *"...holy brethren..."* and again in *verse twelve*, *"...beware, brethren..."*. **This letter to Christians with a Jewish heritage is written to believers as believers!**

The writer of this letter was a good *"...steward of the mysteries of God..." (I Corinthians 4:1)* making certain believers' growth was according to God's design. God's expectations are very clear throughout the New Testament as the Holy Spirit inspired James to write in simple and elegant terms.

> *"Be doers of the word, and not hearers only, deceiving yourselves. For if anyone is a hearer of the word and not a doer, he is like a man observing his natural face in a mirror; for he observes himself, goes away, and immediately forgets what kind of man he was. But he who looks into the perfect law of liberty and continues in it, and is not a forgetful hearer but a doer of the work, this one will be blessed in what he does."* **James 1:22-25**

Diversity of Submission

All believers are expected to be *"...doers of the Word they receive..."*. Being a doer requires skill development in order to make the Word a way of life. The writer of the letter to the Hebrews wrote *"...everyone who partakes only of milk is unskilled (552) in the word of righteousness, for he is a babe..."*.

> **552 apeiros** from *I* (as a neg. particle) and *3984; inexperienced*, i.e. *ignorant*: -- unskilfil.
>
> <u>***Strong's Exhaustive Concordance of the Bible***</u>

Being a *"...doer of the Word..."* or becoming *"...skilled in the Word..."* both have the same fundamental goal: **Make the Word a way of life!** Consider a spiritual illustration; *"...baptized into One body..."*, a basic principle of the doctrine of Christ. As a believer *"...hears this word..."*, receives understanding from the Holy Spirit that we are members of the same body, Christ's body, and submits to this Word, he will begin to connect with other parts of the body as the way he is to live.

Paul was inspired to write about believers being united in practical unity in all of his epistles! Some of the most profound of these writings were to the church at Corinth.

> *"Now I plead with you, brethren, by the name of our Lord Jesus Christ, that you all speak the same thing, and that there be no divisions among you, but that you be perfectly joined together in the same mind and in the same judgment."*
> **I Corinthians 1:10**
>
> *"For as the body is one and has many members, but all the members of that one body, being many, are one body, so also is Christ. For by one Spirit we were all baptized into one*

body -- whether Jews or Greeks, whether slaves or free -- and have all been made to drink into one Spirit. For in fact the body is not one member but many. If the foot should say, 'Because I am not a hand, I am not of the body,' is it therefore not of the body? And if the ear should say, 'Because I am not an eye, I am not of the body,' is it therefore not of the body? If the whole body were an eye, where would be the hearing? If the whole were hearing, where would be the smelling? But now God has set the members, each one of them, in the body just as He pleased. And if they were all one member, where would the body be? But now indeed there are many members, yet one body. And the eye cannot say to the hand, 'I have no need of you'; nor again the head to the feet, 'I have no need of you.' No, much rather, those members of the body which seem to be weaker are necessary. And those members of the body which we think to be less honorable, on these we bestow greater honor; and our unpresentable parts have greater modesty, but our presentable parts have no need. But God composed the body, having given greater honor to that part which lacks it, that there should be no schism in the body, but that the members should have the same care for one another. And if one member suffers, all the members suffer with it; or if one member is honored, all the members rejoice with it." **I Corinthians 12:12-26**

Members of the church, the body of Christ, are ordained to function as one body. As we acknowledge this is the will of the Lord and begin to willingly submit to Jesus as Lord in the matter, we will begin to be concerned about the well-being of the body as Christ's body. This *"...revelation..."* will help motivate us to freely give our knowledge and skill to others. We will actually begin to be *"...teachers..." **(Hebrews 5:12)*** just as the Lord ordained. We will not be vocational ministers called to the role of teacher, but we will be *"...believers teaching other believers..."*.

Diversity of Submission

It is written in **Hebrews 5:12**, *"...For though by this time you ought to be teachers..."*. **How does a believer determine when it is time to teach another believer?** A believer's knowledge of the Word and *"...skill..."* in the use of the Word will determine when he is ready to *"...teach..."* others. This type of understanding is the same as presented in Scripture regarding prophecy, *"...let us prophesy in proportion to our faith..." (**Romans 12:6**)*. A believer can only prophesy according to his proportion of faith. A believer can only teach according to the *knowledge and skill* he himself has. This makes the way we are to be teachers *"...an easy yoke and a light burden..." (**Matthew 11:28-30**)*.

Consider illustrations from the natural world: Parents teach their children to use the mower to cut the lawn or to use the oven to cook a wonderful meal. The parents do not need to fast, pray, or study in order to *"...teach..."* their children the skills with which they themselves as parents are already skilled. *"For though by this time you ought to be teachers..."* is this same type of teaching reference.

A believer is only expected to "...teach..." the knowledge and skills he already has. A skilled believer can easily *"...teach..."* others. However, this *"...teaching..."* process is only possible if the believer who needs to be taught willingly submits himself. A babe-in-Christ *needs* to willingly submit to be *"...trained..."* by another believer so, too, when he is ready to *"...train..."* a believer himself, that believer must willingly submit to him for *"...training..."*. **This is the way of the kingdom.**

This type of *"...teaching..."* establishes a specific type of relationship between believers. As flesh and bone members of Christ's body there are a diversity of relationships between the members, some direct, others indirect. Christ's body is universal, covering the whole earth and even heaven. We still have relationships with those members of Christ's body with whom we have no direct contact because we are all members of Christ's body. Those relationships which are direct, that is relationships with persons with whom we are actually walking personally, will obviously function differently because we walk together practically. We must have a global or universal vision of the body of Christ but allow for diversities of relationships within the body.

Relationships can only be successfully developed through effective communication. Effective communication is only possible by properly identifying roles. This *"...relationship model..."* can be illustrated using a simple diagram.

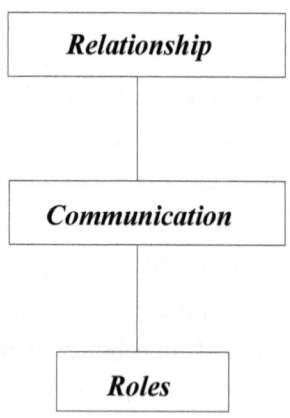

Diversity of Submission

Roles are the foundation for effective communication. Effective communication is the foundation for healthy relationships. Correct practice of this simple *"...relationship model..."* will activate a powerful supernatural principle. Matthew recorded Jesus revealing this principle.

> *"He who receives you receives Me, and he who receives Me receives Him who sent Me. He who receives a prophet in the name of a prophet shall receive a prophet's reward. And he who receives a righteous man in the name of a righteous man shall receive a righteous man's reward. And whoever gives one of these little ones only a cup of cold water in the name of a disciple, assuredly, I say to you, he shall by no means lose his reward."* **Matthew 10:40-42**

Hidden inside these three verses is a secret of the kingdom. Jesus told His disciples, *"...it has been given to you to know the mysteries (secrets or hidden truths) of the kingdom..." (**Matthew 13:11**)*. The Lord desires for us to know and understand the secret contained within these verses and the Holy Spirit is zealous to reveal it.

The mystery revolves around how we receive one another. Although the mystery is not limited to receiving just a righteous man, that will be our focus. Notice in *verse forty one* Jesus said, *"...he who receives a righteous man in the name of a righteous man shall receive a righteous man's reward..."*. Receiving a righteous man in the name of a righteous man is simply receiving a righteous man as a righteous man. The name of a righteous man is ***"...righteous man..."!*** ***Simple!*** But what is the righteous man's reward we are to receive? There are many rewards of the righteous man, but considering only one here will move us forward in our understanding. Consider the epistle James wrote.

Rewards of Heavenly Submission

> *"The effective, fervent prayer of a righteous man avails much. Elijah was a man with a nature like ours, and he prayed earnestly that it would not rain; and it did not rain on the land for three years and six months. And he prayed again, and the heaven gave rain, and the earth produced its fruit."* **James 5:16-18**

Although Elijah was a prophet of the Most High God anointed to walk in the supernatural, the Holy Spirit inspired James to compare the prayer of a righteous man with that of Elijah. It is the will of God for *"...the effective, fervent prayer of a righteous man to avail much..."*, just like the prayers Elijah prayed regarding the rain. If we could only see righteousness as God sees it! If we could see ourselves as righteous like God sees us. If we could see one another as righteous like God sees all of the redeemed.

The result of the *"...effective, fervent prayer that avails much..."* is a reward. Even if we restrict the *"...reward of a righteous man..."* to only *"...prayer that avails much..."*; **that is an amazing *"...reward...*"!** According to the Word of the Lord, *"...he who receives a righteous man in the name of a righteous man shall receive a righteous man's reward..."*. That means if we receive a righteous man as a righteous man, when he prays for us, his *"...effective, fervent prayer..."* will avail much on our behalf. According to the inspired writing of James the *"...effective, fervent prayer of a righteous man avails much..."* is comparable to Elijah's prayers. Oh, the vile corruption of the enemy who has endeavored to deceive us in an effort to steal the power of our righteousness! God has made ***us*** the *"...righteousness of God in Christ Jesus..." **(II Corinthians 5:21)*** which would make our prayers powerful if we had *"...revelation..."* of our rightesousness and prayed accordingly!

Diversity of Submission

While this truth is *"...legal..."* in God, it is all too often not *"...practical..."* in the church. Consider a natural world illustration: When a man and a woman enter holy matrimony, they become legally one in the eyes of God and our government. However, the legal unity of the marriage does not always equate to practical unity. The husband and wife may be legally one but not practically walking in unity.

So, too, it is with righteousness. All born again persons have *"...become the righteousness of God in Christ..."* (**II Corinthians 5:21**) legally, but all born again persons do not necessarily walk in a righteous manner and may not even see themselves as righteous. How a person sees himself in his heart will determine how he is and how he will walk. Consider the wisdom of God provided through Scripture in this matter.

> *"...as he (a man) thinks in his heart, so is he..."*
> **Proverbs 23:6,7**

> *"As in water face reflects face, so a man's heart reveals the man."* **Proverbs 27:19**

> *"Out of the abundance of the heart the mouth speaks."*
> **Matthew 12:34; Luke 6:45**

In order for a born again person to experience the benefits of his righteousness he must have received *"...revelation..."* of *"...righteousness..."* from the Holy Spirit and walk as a righteous man. In order for the church to experience a *"...righteous man's reward..."* we must understand righteousness, see ourselves as righteous, and receive one another as righteous men. Any lack of any these three things in our lives will be very problematic!

The will of God is absolutely clear, *"...the natural man does not receive the things of the Spirit of God, for they are foolishness to him; nor can he know them, because they are spiritually discerned..." (context **I Corinthians 2:9-14**)*. Natural man's mental assent to the Word of God will not produce the supernatural results God intends. We must have divine revelation from God the Holy Spirit given to and received by our spirit. Paul admonished Timothy concerning these matters regarding perilous times and perilous men.

> *"But know this, that in the last days perilous times will come: For men will be lovers of themselves, lovers of money, boasters, proud, blasphemers, disobedient to parents, unthankful, unholy, unloving, slanderers, without self-control, brutal, despisers of good, traitors, headstrong, haughty, lovers of pleasure rather than lovers of God, having a form of godliness but denying its power. And from such people turn away! For of this sort are those who creep into households and make captives of gullible women loaded down with sins, led away by various lusts, **always learning and never able to come to the knowledge of the truth...**" **II Timothy 3:1-7***

Even though believers may learn and come to the knowledge of the truth, that doesn't guarantee they will walk in the truth as a way of life. The church at Laodicea serves as a wonderful illustration of how people began correctly but later chose a way of error. We saw how the Laodicean church went *"...from submission to unsubmission..."* in **Chapter One, page 14**. We must avoid this trap.

Proverbs 4:23 instructs us to *"Keep your heart with all diligence, for out of it spring the issues of life."*. As we guard our heart with all diligence remaining spiritually minded, we will see ourselves and one another as *"...the righteousness of God in Christ Jesus..."*. This

Diversity of Submission

was the first *"...role..."* assigned to us as we entered Christ at the time of our new birth: *"...the righteousness of God in Christ Jesus..."*. Any communication we have with one another without properly identifying this role will be ineffective leading to relationships less than the Lord has ordained.

All roles within the church begin with our being *"...the righteousness of God in Christ Jesus..."*. All communication must emerge from proper identification and acceptance of this role. Only when we see ourselves and one another as *"...the righteousness of God in Christ Jesus..."* will our relationships flourish within the church! With *"...diversity of submission..."*, that is submission *"...over or under..."* another believer, *"...righteous believer..."* must be the foundation!

Rewards of Heavenly Submission

Chapter Six

Submission to Governing Authorities

During the time of Jesus' arrest in the Garden of Gethsemane a significant event occurred inspiring Jesus to identify the importance of submission to governing authorities in His own life and ministry. Peter pulled his sword and struck the servant of the high priest cutting off his ear. Jesus then spoke this important word to Peter,

> "Put your sword in its place, for all who take the sword will perish by the sword. Or do you think that I cannot now pray to My Father, and He will provide Me with more than twelve legions of angels? **How then could the Scriptures be fulfilled, that it must happen thus?"** Matthew 26:52-54

Although Jesus made it clear He could have prayed to His Father and received heavenly deliverance from this arrest, He also made it clear His submission to the governing authorities was necessary in order to fulfill His purpose.

After Jesus' betrayal and arrest in the Garden the soldiers led Him to the Sanhedrin Council, the Jewish religious authorities. This Council sent Him to Pontius Pilate, Governor of Judaea. Pilate sent Him to Herod, Tetrarch or King of Galilee. Herod sent Jesus back to Pilate. Even though there were many social, religious, and political issues involved in why Jesus was shuffled from one authority to another, all governing authorities had one

Rewards of Heavenly Submission

thing in common: They were ignorant of the *"...truth..."* that **Jesus' kingdom was not of this world!** Jesus expressed this heavenly mystery openly to Pilate,

> *"My kingdom is not of this world. If My kingdom were of this world, My servants would fight, so that I should not be delivered to the Jews; but now My kingdom is not from here."* **John 18:36**

Even though these words simply and clearly expressed the truth, Pilate did not understand. Jesus spoke heavenly revelation, but Pilate could not receive it. It is as if he did not even hear Jesus' words. After Jesus had given Pilate this heavenly revelation, Pilate asked Jesus a question which Jesus refused to answer.

Frustrated by Jesus' non-response, Pilate believed it was by *"...his..."* power as a governing authority that Jesus would be crucified or released, so he asked Jesus these rhetorical questions,

> *"Are you not speaking to me? Do You not know that I have power to crucify You, and power to release You?"*
> **John 19:10**

Jesus' response adds another layer to our understanding.

> *You could have no power at all against Me unless it had been given you from above."* **John 19:11**

Here Jesus was presenting distinction and rank among kingdoms. The governing authorities of all kingdoms are below the authority of the kingdom of God. Any authority Pilate had against Christ was only because it *"...was given him from above...".*

Submission To Governing Authorities

The governing authorities of this world and the rulers of this age played important parts in bringing Jesus' purpose on earth to its finale. Jesus introduced this fact when He admonished Peter in the Garden of Gethsemane regarding the use of the sword *(Matthew 26:52-54)*. Paul expanded this understanding in his letter to the church at Corinth. He wrote about speaking the wisdom of God in a mystery...

> *"...the hidden wisdom which God ordained before the ages for our glory, which none of the rulers of this age knew; for had they known, they would not have crucified the Lord of glory..."* **I Corinthians 2:7,8**

Pilate as the governing authority in this world actually had the power to crucify or release a prisoner. But even though it was Pilate who gave the order for Jesus to be crucified, the motivation to crucify Jesus came from the governing authorities of the kingdom of darkness. Paul's inspired writing said *"...the rulers of this age...crucified the Lord of glory..."*. Even though human governing authority and the rulers of this age were both involved in ordering Jesus to be crucified, Jesus spoke very plainly that no one had the power nor authority to take His life from Him, only He had the power to lay it down.

> *"I am the good shepherd; and I know My sheep, and am known by My own. As the Father knows Me, even so I know the Father; and I lay down My life for the sheep. And other sheep I have which are not of this fold; them also I must bring, and they will hear My voice; and there will be one flock and one shepherd. Therefore My Father loves Me, because I lay down My life that I may take it again. No one takes it from Me, but I lay it down, and I have power to take it again. This command I have received from My Father."*
> **John 10:14-18**

Rewards of Heavenly Submission

It was Jesus' submission to the governing authorities who gave the order for His crucifixion that made a way for Him to actually be crucified! Crucifixion was the finale of His earthly ministry and necessary to provide the eternal redemption for all mankind. Jesus had submitted to this plan as God the Word before He partook of flesh and blood becoming the man Jesus. Now that the Word was clothed in flesh, Jesus as a man remained submitted to the plan of redemption. Revelation is clear for us to be able to understand Jesus' submission to governing authorities in the matter of crucifixion.

> *No one could take Jesus' life unless He submitted to it!*

Now, does the Lord of Glory have any specific "...will..." regarding our submitting to governing authorities? As we consider our possible submission to governing authorities, it will be helpful to remember God is Sovereign, and all other governing authorities are below Him.

"*If God be for us, who can be against us?*"
Romans 8:31

"*He who is in you is greater than he who is in the world.*"
I John 4:4

Scripture provides two relevant instructions to believers written by John and Paul which help move us forward in answering the question regarding the Lord's will for our submitting to governing authorities.

Submission To Governing Authorities

> *"He who says he abides in Him ought himself also to walk just as He walked."* **I John 2:6**

> *"Let this mind be in you which was also in Christ Jesus, who, being in the form of God, did not consider it robbery to be equal with God, but made Himself of no reputation, taking the form of a bond-servant, He humbled Himself and became obedient to the point of death, even the death of the cross..."* context **Philippians 2:5-11**

Because Jesus submitted to governing authorities, we, too, are to submit to them. He is our pattern. This is the will of God! However, we need clear understanding to determine if there are specific instructions or restrictions to our submission, or do we simply submit *carte blanche*?

Jesus often spoke directly and in parables about the *"...religiosity..."* of the Pharisees and Sadducees. Because of this many of these Jewish leaders sought ways to trap Jesus in order to *"...entangle Him in His talk..."*.

> *"Then the Pharisees went and plotted how they might entangle Him in His talk. And they sent to Him their disciples with the Herodians, saying, 'Teacher, we know that You are true, and teach the way of God in truth; nor do You care about anyone, for You do not regard the person of men. Tell us, therefore, what do You think? Is it lawful to pay taxes to Caesar, or not?' But Jesus perceived their wickedness, and said, 'Why do you test Me, you hypocrites? Show Me the tax money.' So they brought Him a denarius. And He said to them, 'Whose image and inscription is this?' They said to Him, 'Caesar's.' And He said to them, 'Render therefore to Caesar the things that are Caesar's and to God the things that are God's.' When they had heard these words, they marveled, and left Him and went their way."*
> **Matthew 22:15-22**

Rewards of Heavenly Submission

Jesus' response to their attempt to *"...entangle Him..."* provides us with revelation which will serve as foundation upon which we can begin to build understanding regarding our submission to governing authorities. Notice the subtle, but unmistakable, identification Jesus makes distinguishing kingdoms: Caesar's kingdom and God's kingdom. This distinction will provide us with a standard whereby we can compare kingdoms to determine whether they are man's or God's prior to our decision to submit to governing authorities.

This distinction is so important it will help guide the entirety of our lives in Christ. All believers must be able to identify the kingdom of God in contrast to all other kingdoms and governing authorities. A natural world illustration using this type of contrast comes from the *United States Secret Service* in relation to identifying counterfeit money. According to the official *United States Secret Service* website:

> "The public has a role in maintaining the integrity of U.S. currency. You can help guard against the threat from counterfeiters by becoming more familiar with United States currency.
>
> Look at the money you receive. Compare a suspect note with a genuine note of the same denomination and series, paying attention to the quality of printing and paper characteristics. Look for differences, not similarities."

Secret Service agents are trained to detect counterfeit money by becoming so familiar with real money they can easily identify the *"...differences..."* in the counterfeit from the real. Christians must be trained to become so familiar with the real kingdom they can easily identify the differences in the counterfeit from the real. Jesus commanded us...

Submission To Governing Authorities

> *"...Seek first the kingdom of God and His righteousness, and all these things (the things the Gentiles seek) will be added to you..."* **Matthew 6:33**

Any believer who has not submitted to Jesus' command to *"...seek first the kingdom of God and His righteousness..."* will be an easy target for the deceiving devices of the enemy in which to be entangled. Comparative contrasts are such an important part of the Christian life, God the Holy Spirit inspired much to be written about them.

Paul admonished the church at Galatia,

> *"I marvel that you are turning away so soon from Him who called you in the grace of Christ, to a different gospel, which is not another; but there are some who trouble you and want to pervert the gospel of Christ. But even if we, or an angel from heaven, preach any other gospel to you than what we have preached to you, let him be accursed. As we have said before, so now I say again, if anyone preaches any other gospel to you than what you have received, let him be accursed..."* **Galatians 1:6-9**

In this admonition Paul told the church to use the gospel *"...you have received..."* which *"...called you in the grace of Christ..."* as the standard by which to compare any other gospel preached. God the Holy Spirit is so adamant in the matter he inspired Paul to write in extreme terms to persuade the Galatians. Paul wrote, *"...even if we, or an angel from heaven, preach any other gospel to you than what we have preached to you, let him be accursed..."*. The issue is so vital Paul was inspired to repeat the very same statement he just wrote, *"...so now I say again, if anyone preaches any other gospel to you than what you have received, let him be accursed..."*. Obviously, the intent was if *"...another gospel..."* was preached to them, they were not to receive it if it did not accurately compare to the gospel which *"...called you in the grace of Christ...".* The extreme lengths Paul was inspired to write in this matter are almost unimaginable.

John wrote an encouraging word in his first epistle about a heavenly provision for believers to be able to know truth from untruth.

> *"Little children, it is the last hour; and as you have heard that the Antichrist is coming, even now many antichrists have come, by which we know that it is the last hour. They went out from us, but they were not of us; for if they had been of us, they would have continued with us; but they went out that they might be made manifest, that none of them were of us. But you have an anointing from the Holy One, and you know all things. I have not written to you because you do not know the truth, but because you know it, and that no lie is of the truth. Who is a liar but he who denies that Jesus is the Christ? He is antichrist who denies the Father and the Son. Whoever denies the Son does not have the Father either; he who acknowledges the Son has the Father also. Therefore let that abide in you which you heard from the beginning. If what you heard from the beginning abides in you, you also will abide in the Son and in the Father. And this is the promise that He has promised us --- eternal life. These things I have written to you concerning those who try to deceive you. But the anointing which you have received from Him abides in you, and you do not need that anyone teach you; but as the same anointing teaches you concerning all things, and is true, and is not a lie, and just as it has taught you, you will abide in Him."* **I John 2:18-27**

Abba, our Father, has provided the *"...anointing..."* who *"...abides in you, and you do not need that anyone teach you; but as the same anointing teaches you concerning all things...".* It is the will of God that we know the difference between truth, lies, and all things

Submission To Governing Authorities

antichrist. Since God designed the new covenant to be lived in His ability rather than our own ability, we cannot know as we ought to know in our own ability. God loves us so much He has given us the *"...anointing..."* as His holy provision so we may know truth from lies and all things antichrist.

We know this ***Truth*** about the Lord's will regarding our submitting to governing authorities:

1. *We know to distinguish the kingdom of man from the kingdom of God prior to submission to governing authorities.*

2. *We know to use the gospel which "...called you in the grace of Christ..." as the standard by which we contrast anything else preached to us.*

3. *We know we have the "...anointing..." from God so that as "...the same anointing teaches us concerning all things..." we will know Truth as our Standard!*

The priority of our submission is to God above all else! Christ as ***Truth*** is the Standard whereby we measure any other input into our lives! If any governing authorities present anything contrary to the governing authorities of the kingdom of God, we must not submit to them. ***Christ is preeminent!***

> *"He (God the Father) put all things under His (Jesus') feet, and gave Him to be head over all things to the church, which is His body, the fullness of Him who fills all in all."*
> **Ephesians 1:22-23**

> *"And He (Jesus) is the head of the body, the church, who is the beginning, the firstborn from the dead, that in all things He may have the preeminence."* **Colossians 1:18**

Rewards of Heavenly Submission

An example of governing authorities presenting something in direct violation to what Scripture clearly presents as the will of God is the national debate in our nation over same-sex marriages. Scripture speaks directly to this particular subject.

> *"For the wrath of God is revealed from heaven against all ungodliness and unrighteousness of men, who suppress the truth in unrighteousness, because what may be known of God is manifest in them, for God has shown it to them. For since the creation of the world His invisible attributes are clearly seen, being understood by the things that are made, even His eternal power and Godhead, so that they are without excuse, because, although they knew God, they did not glorify Him as God, nor were thankful, but became futile in their thoughts, and their foolish hearts were darkened. Professing to be wise, they became fools, and changed the glory of the incorruptible God into an image made like corruptible man -- and birds and four-footed animals and creeping things. Therefore God also gave them up to uncleanness, in the lusts of their hearts, to dishonor their bodies among themselves, who exchanged the truth of God for the lie, and worshipped and served the creature rather than the Creator, who is blessed forever. Amen. For this reason God gave them up to vile passions. For even their **women exchanged the natural use for what is against nature. Likewise also the men, leaving the natural use of the woman, burned in their lust for one another, men with men committing what is shameful**, and receiving in themselves the penalty of their error which was due. And even as they did not like to retain God in their knowledge, God gave them over to a debased mind, to do those things which are not fitting; being filled with all unrighteousness, sexual immorality, wickedness, covetousness, maliciousness; full of envy, murder, strife, deceit, evil-mindedness, they are whisperers, backbiters, haters of God, violent, proud, boasters, inventors of evil things, disobedient to parents, undiscerning, untrustworthy, unloving, unforgiving, unmerciful; who, knowing the righteous judgment of God, that those who practice such things are deserving of death."* **Romans 1:18-32**

Submission To Governing Authorities

> *"Do you not know that the unrighteous will not inherit the kingdom of God? Do not be deceived.* **Neither fornicators, nor idolaters, nor adulterers, nor homosexuals, nor sodomites, nor thieves, nor covetous, nor drunkards, nor revilers, nor extortioners will inherit the kingdom of God.** *And such were some of you. But you were washed, but you were sanctified, but you were justified in the name of the Lord Jesus and by the Spirit of God."* **I Corinthians 6:9-11**

No born again believer is required to submit to the legality nor acceptance of same-sex marriages simply because the governing authorities of a nation require it. Peter wrote an important word regarding submission to the ordinance of man.

> *"Beloved, I beg you as sojourners and pilgrims, abstain from fleshly lusts which war against the soul, having your conduct honorable among the Gentiles, that when they speak against you as evildoers, they may, by your good works which they observe, glorify God in the day of visitation. Therefore submit yourselves to every ordinance of man for the Lord's sake, whether to the king as supreme, or to governors, as to those who are sent by him for the punishment of evildoers and for the praise of those who do good. For this is the will of God, that by doing good you may put to silence the ignorance of foolish men -- as free, yet not using liberty as a cloak for vice, but as bondservants of God. Honor all people. Love the brotherhood. Fear God. Honor the king."*
> **I Peter 5:11-17**

We are to *"...submit yourselves to every ordinance of man for the Lord's sake, whether to the king as supreme, or to governors..."* and to *"...Honor the king...".* However, Jesus as Lord is our priority. Anything which violates what He has clearly revealed as a violation of His will is not required! Consider an illustration from Scripture regarding the *"...apostles of the Lamb..."* being commanded by religious governing authorities not to do what the apostles knew to be the will of God.

Peter had prayed for *"...a certain man lame from his mother's womb was carried whom they laid daily at the gate of the temple which is called Beautiful..."* and the man was healed *(Entire context Acts 3:1-4:31).* Peter and John were taken before the Sanhedrin Council to give account for their actions, not only for the lame man being healed, but for *"...preaching Jesus the resurrection from the dead...".* The Council...

> *"...called them (Peter and John) and commanded them not to speak at all nor teach in the name of Jesus. But Peter and John answered and said to them, 'Whether it is right in the sight of God to listen to you more than to God, you judge. For we cannot but speak the things which we have seen and heard.' So when they had further threatened them, they let them go, finding no way of punishing them, because of the people, since they all glorified God for what had been done..."* **Acts 4:18-21**

Under these same conditions and in this same environment, the apostles having been let go by the Sanhedrin Council continued to preach in boldness and authority. The apostles were arrested again and brought before the same religious governing authorities. The high priest asked them,

> *"... 'Did we not strictly command you not to teach in this name? And look, you have filled Jerusalem with your doctrine, and intend to bring this Man's blood on us!' But Peter and the other apostles answered and said: 'We ought to obey God rather than men. The God of our fathers raised up Jesus whom you murdered by hanging on a tree. Him God has highly exalted to His right hand to be Prince and*

Submission To Governing Authorities

*Savior, to give repentance to Israel and forgiveness of sins. And we are His witnesses to these things, and so also is the Holy Spirit whom God has given to those who obey Him.' When they heard this, they were furious and plotted to kill them. Then one in the council stood up, a Pharisee named Gamaliel, a teacher of the law held in respect by all the people, and commanded them to put the apostles outside for a little while. And he said to them: 'Men of Israel, take heed to yourselves what you intend to do regarding these men. For some time ago Theudas rose up, claiming to be somebody. A number of men, about four hundred, joined him. He was slain, and all who obeyed him were scattered and came to nothing. After this man Judas of Galilee rose up in the days of the census, and drew away many people after him. He also perished, and all who obeyed him were dispersed. And now I say to you, keep away from these men and let them work alone; for if this plan or this work is of men, it will come to nothing; but if it is of God, you cannot overthrow it -- lest you even be found to fight against God.' And they agreed with him, and **when they had called for the apostles and beaten them, they commanded that they should not speak in the name of Jesus, and let them go**. So they departed from the presence of the council, rejoicing that they were counted worthy to suffer shame for His name. And daily in the temple, and in every house, they did not cease teaching and preaching Jesus as the Christ." **Acts 5:28-42**

The apostles refused submission to these governing authorities because their directive was a violation of the will of God. The apostles chose *"...to obey God rather than men.."!*

The governing authorities of the kingdom of God are always priority over the governing authorities of any other kingdom!

Rewards of Heavenly Submission

Chapter Seven

Submission to Spiritual Authorities

> *There are three spiritual laws required for the successful operation of the church!*

1. *Heavenly submission to Jesus as Lord is priority.*

2. *Jesus as Lord, head of the church, His own body, is preeminent in all things to the church.*

3. *Every relationship within the church is founded on the individual role of righteous believer.*

> <u>Note</u>: Heavenly submission is submission according to the will of God!

No matter what *"...role..."* any member of Christ's body may have these three laws must be applied to everyone. In this dispensation Jesus' role as Lord is only rewarding for those who willingly submit to Him. **Submission within His kingdom is absolutely essential!** If the church is not submitted to Jesus as Lord, a subtle type of *"...anarchy..."* will rule as demonstrated in Israel when there was no king, *"...everyone does what was right in his own eyes..." **(Judges 17:6)**.

We desire revelation from God upon which to base our submission to spiritual authorities. Writing by inspiration of the Holy Spirit, Peter wrote in his first epistle, *"...as newborn*

Rewards of Heavenly Submission

babes, desire the pure milk of the word, that you may grow thereby..." ***(I Peter 2:2)***. Every born again person enters the new covenant as a *"...newborn babe..."*. There are no exceptions! **Growth** is inextricably linked to intake of *"...the pure milk of the word..."*.

There is an attribute relevant to all infants: ***unskilled!***

> *"...everyone who partakes only of milk is **unskilled (552)** in the word of righteousness, for he is a babe. But solid food belongs to those who are of full age, that is, those who by reason of use have their senses exercised to discern both good and evil..."* **Hebrews 5:13,14**
>
> ***552 apeiros*** from ***I*** (as a neg. particle) and ***3984***; inexperienced, i.e. ignorant: -- unskillful.
>
> <u>**Strong's Exhaustive Concordance of the Bible**</u>

Scripture specifically states *"...those who are of full age, that is, those who by reason of use have their senses exercised to discern both good and evil..."*. The ability *"...to discern both good and evil..."* comes with *"...the exercise of senses..."*, in other words *"...experience..."*. Every newborn babe *"...partakes only of milk..."* because he is *"...unskilled in the word of righteousness, for he is a babe..."*. That is, every newborn babe is *"...inexperienced..."* in the word of righteousness meaning his spiritual skills are not yet developed; ***he is unskilled!***

Because Jesus taught many invisible spiritual truths using visible natural illustrations, we, too, can use this same teaching format. A natural infant has not yet developed his physical or mental skills. Scripture has already shown us a spiritual infant has not yet developed his spiritual skills. Both natural and

Submission To Spiritual Authorities

spiritual infants must have oversight to help them grow properly. Lack of proper oversight will produce dire consequences in either.

In 1954 William Golding, a Nobel Prize-winning author, wrote the novel **_Lord of the Flies_**. The story revolves around a group of school boys who were involved in a plane crash and forced to live on an uninhabited island. These boys tried to *"... oversee..."* themselves with disastrous results. They were not sufficiently mature nor did they have adequate resources to provide the necessary oversight for them to grow properly.

We were not crashed nor forced to live in Christ! We submitted to Jesus as Lord and were baptized into Him by the Most High God. The same God who baptized us into Christ made us flesh and bone members of Christ's body and appointed Him to be Head over us. He also gave Jesus *"...all authority in heaven and on earth..." **(Matthew 28:18)*** so He would have the resources necessary to fulfill His role. From His position as Lord and Head over His own body, Jesus has provided for us...

> *"...He Himself gave some to be apostles, some prophets, some evangelists, and some pastors and teachers, for the equipping of the saints for the work of the ministry, for the edifying of the body of Christ, **till we all come to the unity of the faith and of the knowledge of the Son of God, to a perfect man, to the measure of the stature of the fullness of Christ, that we should be no longer children,** tossed to and fro and carried about with every wind of doctrine, by the trickery of men, in the cunning craftiness of deceitful plotting, but speaking the truth in love, **may grow up in all things into Him who is the head** -- **Christ --** from whom the whole body, joined and knit together by what every joint supplies, according to the effective working by which every part does its share, causes growth of the body for the edifying of itself in love." **Ephesians 4:11-16***

Rewards of Heavenly Submission

These ministries have been given *"...till we all come to the unity of the faith and of the knowledge of the Son of God, to a perfect man, to the measure of the stature of the fullness of Christ, that we should be no longer children..."*. The length of time the ministries have been given translates into a **statement of purpose**: To help the saints grow so they *"...should be no longer children..."* but mature into *"...a perfect man, to the measure of the stature of the fullness of Christ..."*. The saints grow and mature through the *"...knowledge of the Son of God..."*.

The ministries each freely receive revelation of Christ and are ordained to freely give what they have received to the sons of God as the means for the sons to grow. This knowledge of the Son of God must become the way the saints live: The saints must be *"...doers..."* of the word they receive *(James 1:22-25)*.

In Peter's first epistle he addressed the role of those who *"...shepherd (tend, feed, or rule) the flock of God..."*.

> *"The elders who are among you I exhort, I who am a fellow elder and a witness of the sufferings of Christ, and also a partaker of the glory that will be revealed: Shepherd (4165) the flock of God which is among you, serving as overseers (1983), not by compulsion but willingly, not for dishonest gain but eagerly; nor as being lords (2634) over those entrusted to you, but being examples (5179) to the flock; and when the Chief Shepherd appears, you will receive the crown of glory that does not fade away."* **I Peter 5:1-5**

4165 poimaino from *4166*; to *tend* as a shepherd (or fig. *supervisor*): -- feed (cattle), rule.

1983 episkopeo from *1909* and *4648*; to *oversee*; by impl. to *beware*; -- look diligently, take the oversight.

Submission To Spiritual Authorities

2634 katakurieno from *2596* and *2601*; *to lord against*, i.e. *control, subjugate*: -- exercise dominion over (lordship), be lord over, overcome.

5179 tupos from *5280*; a *die* (as *struck*), i.e. (by impl.) a *stamp* or *scar*; by anal. a *shape*, i.e. a *statue*, (fig.) *style* or *resemblance*; spec. a *sampler* ("type"), i.e. a *model* (for imitation) or *instance* (for warning): -- en- (ex-) ample, fashion, figure, form, manner, pattern, print.

<u>*Strong's Exhaustive Concordance of the Bible*</u>

Paul presented the same type of understanding as Peter regarding his ministerial role to the saints in his letter to the church at Corinth.

"Imitate (3402) me, just as I also imitate (3402) Christ."
I Corinthians 11:1

3402 mimetes from *3401*; an *imitator*: -- follower.

<u>*Strong's Exhaustive Concordance of the Bible*</u>

Peter's admonition to the *"...elders..."* included strong contrasts between *"...shepherds (4165)..."*, *"...overseers (1983)..."*, *"...examples (5179)..."*, and *"...lords (2634)..."*. No ministry other than Christ **has been given** to provide any type of *"...lordship..."* over the flock. Ministers **are** *"...leaders..."*, but as *"...examples, patterns, or models..."* to the saints, just as Paul instructed the church at Corinth to *"...**imitate (3402) me, just as I also imitate (3402) Christ**..."*.

The writer of the letter to the Hebrews presented a revelation regarding the relationship the saints are to have with those who *"...rule..."* in the church.

Rewards of Heavenly Submission

*"Remember those **who rule (2233) over you**, who have spoken the word of God to you, whose faith follow, considering the outcome of their conduct."* **Hebrews 13:7**

2233 **hegeomai** mid. of a (presumed) strengthened form of *71;* to *lead,* i.e. *command* (with official authority); fig. to *deem,* i.e. *consider:* -- account, (be) chief, count, esteem, governor, judge, have the rule over, suppose, think.

<u>**Strong's Exhaustive Concordance of the Bible**</u>

There are ministers within the church who are to *"...**have the rule over**..."* the sons of God but in a very prescribed manner. Application of the *"...three spiritual laws..."* required for the successful operation of the church will keep us safely within the revelation of those who *"...**have the rule over**..."* us.

1. *Heavenly submission to Jesus as Lord is priority, therefore no other role of ministry can ever become priority in the church.*

2. *Jesus as Lord, head of the church, His own body, is preeminent in all things to the church, therefore no role of ministry can ever rise to a place of preeminence in the church.*

3. *Every relationship within the church is founded on the individual role of righteous believer, therefore no role of ministry can ever stand independent from the role of righteous believer.*

Submission To Spiritual Authorities

The first spiritual authority to whom believers submit within the church, after they have submitted to the authority of Jesus as Lord, are the ministers responsible to *"...feed..."* the flock of God. An extremely sensitive and important understanding is required to keep error from entering the relationship of submission between believers and ministers.

The type of submission given to ministers by believers is specifically confined to the ministers' gifting and calling within the church. The enemy has tried to corrupt the revelation of *"...submission..."* by attempting to expand the jurisdiction of the minister. Ministers can counsel a believer, pray with a believer, and provide a believer Holy Spirit inspired *"...words of knowledge..."* or *"...words of wisdom..."* about a particular matter in the believer's life. However, they cannot become a substitute for any believers' personal relationship with Jesus as Lord or the Holy Spirit as teacher and guide. No such submission is required nor allowed!

James wrote about those who *"...become teachers...".*

> *"My brethren, let not many of you become teachers, knowing that we shall receive a stricter judgment (2917)."* **James 3:1**
>
> *2917 krima* from *2919* a decision (the function or the effect, for or against ["crime"]): -- avenge, condemned, condemnation, damnation, + go to law, judgment.
>
> <u>**Strong's Exhaustive Concordance of the Bible**</u>

It has already been stated in *Chapter Three, Submission Between Believers, page 29:*

Rewards of Heavenly Submission

> "All submission between believers within the church must begin with each individual believers' submission to Jesus as Lord! The next step of submission must be believer to believer not believer to minister! All relationships in the church are to be founded on life as believers, first believer to Christ, then believer to believer, and only then believer to minister."

Understanding the statement, "...All relationships in the church are to be founded on life as believers, first believer to Christ, then believer to believer, and only then believer to minister.", is essential for us to understand *James 3:1*. Believers are responsible to submit to ministers God has set in the church as the spiritual authorities who *"...feed..."* the flock. However, the priority of this submission is believer to believer, then believer to minister.

The *"...stricter judgment..."* about which James wrote for those who *"...become teachers..."* is for their role as teachers, not their role as righteous believers. The role of righteous believer is the foundation for all other roles anyone may have within the church. The *"...life..."* of any believer who may become a *"...teacher..."* is still to be measured by the righteousness of God in Christ. The role of teacher does not transcend the role of righteous believer. No matter what ministerial role a believer may have the **"...foundation..."** for, and ultimately the **"...priority..."** of, all connections believers have with ministers is believer to righteous believer.

There are three *"....different..."* categories of *"...teachers..."* in the New Testament: Those who are called to the ministry of teacher *(I Corinthians 12:28-31; Ephesians 4:11)*, those who are appointed to the role of elder who may *"...labor in the word and doc-*

trine..." *(I Timothy 5:17)*, and all believers *"...for by this time you ought to be teachers..." (Hebrews 5:12)*. It is extremely difficult to imagine that *James 3:1* *"...let not many of you become teachers..."* is admonishing any believer not to enter the ministry of *"...teacher..."* to which God is calling him. The admonition more aptly fits those who may *"... labor in the word and doctrine..."* from their appointed role of elder. It is also difficult to imagine that *James 3:1* is admonishing believers not to teach the word and skills with which they themselves are knowledgeable and skilled. However, James' admonition needs to be considered by everyone within the church who *"...teaches..."* the Word of God! Anyone who teachers must have the fear of the Lord be the beginning of all we teach!

Other spiritual authorities to whom believers need to submit are elders, deacons, and anyone appointed to fulfill a role of leadership within the church. The jurisdiction of each type of spiritual authority is confined to the specific area within the church over which the person has been set. An example would be the first seven deacons chosen to oversee the distribution of goods to the widows in the church at Jerusalem *(Acts 6:1-7)*.

The authority of these seven deacons was limited as deacons to the distribution of goods to the widows. Anyone having need of distribution of goods or complaint about such distribution needed to submit to those seven deacons who had been given heavenly approval and authority to be responsible for the distribution. However, outside of the scope of the specific responsibility of distribution of goods to the widows of the church the deacons had no jurisdiction other than righteous believers.

Rewards of Heavenly Submission

Chapter Eight

Submission in Marriage

> *"All Scripture is given by inspiration of God, and is profitable for doctrine, for reproof, for correction, for instruction in righteousness, that the man of God may be complete, thoroughly equipped for every good work."*
> **II Timothy 3:16,17**

Anyone who believes *"...All Scripture is given by inspiration of God..."* accepts the information contained within Scripture as what God has chosen to reveal to us in written form. Moses told the children of Israel, *"The secret things belong to the Lord our God, but those things which are revealed belong to us and to our children forever..."* **Deuteronomy 29:29**. Accepting the authenticity of Scripture as the inspired word of God is essential for all born again people.

In the beginning, when God was involved in the creation process, after *"...He formed man of the dust of the ground, and breathed into his nostrils the breath of life; and man became a living being..." **(Genesis 2:7)**,* then God said, *"it is not good that man should be alone; I will make him a helper comparable to him..." **(Genesis 2:18)**.* And so Scripture says...

> *"And the Lord God caused a deep sleep to fall on Adam, and he slept; and He took one of his ribs, and closed up the flesh in its place. Then the rib which the Lord God had taken from man (120) He made into a woman (802), and He brought her to the man. And Adam said:*

Rewards of Heavenly Submission

> '*This is now bone of my bones and flesh of my flesh; she shall be called Woman (802), because she was taken out of Man (376).*'
>
> *Therefore a man (376) shall leave his father and mother and be joined to his wife (802), and they shall become one flesh. And they were both naked, the man (120) and his wife (802), and were not ashamed.*" **Genesis 2:21-25**
>
> **120 'adam** from *119*; *ruddy*, i.e. a *human being* (an individual or the species, *mankind*, etc.): -- x another, + hypocrite, + common sort, x low, man (mean, of low degree), person.
>
> **802 'ishshah** fem.of *376* or *582*; irregular plur. *nashiym*; a *woman* (used in the same wide sense as *582*): -- [adulter]ess, each, every, female, x many, + none, one, + together, wife, woman. Often unexpressed in English.
>
> **376 'iysh** contr. for *582* [or perh. rather from an unused root mean. to *be extant*]; a *man* as an individual or a male person; often used as an adjunct to a more definite term (and in such cases frequently not expressed in translation): -- also, another, any (man), a certain, + champion, consent, each, every (one), fellow, [foot-, husband] man, (good-, great, mighty) man, he, high (degree), him (that is), husband, man [-kind], + none, one, people, person, + steward, what (man) soever, whoso (-ever), worthy. Comp. 802.
>
> <u>**Strong's Exhaustive Concordance of the Bible**</u>

"*...Not wanting Adam to be alone...*" and "*...making him a helper comparable to him...*" was God's introduction of "*...marriage...*" to mankind on the earth. God's design for marriage is: A man "*...leaving his father and mother and being joined to his wife (a woman)...*". This is the will of God as "*...revealed...*" by inspiration of God in Scripture.

Submission in Marriage

When God sent His Word into the earth to be clothed in flesh as the baby Jesus, it marked the beginning of the end of the old covenant. Jesus' presence on the earth heralded the introduction of a new covenant. The old covenant was based on the outward man. The new covenant is based on the inward man. Paul wrote of the stark contrast between *"...our outward man..."* and *"...our inward man..."* in his letter to the church at Corinth *(II Corinthians 4:16)*.

> *"We do not lose heart. Even though our outward man is perishing, yet the inward man is being renewed day by day. For our light affliction, which is but for a moment, is working for us a far more exceeding and eternal weight of glory, while we do not look at the things which are seen, but at the things which are not seen. For the things which are seen are temporary, but the things which are not seen are eternal."* ***II Corinthians 4:16-18***

The *"...eternal redemption..." (Hebrews 9:12)* Jesus died to provide gave mankind opportunity to partake of the new covenant and to enter a spiritual relationship with God Himself! Every person who avails himself of this opportunity and accepts Jesus as Lord becomes a new creation by being born again. Not as Nicodemus asked, *"How can a man be born when he is old? Can he enter a second time into his mother's womb and be born?" (John 3:4)*, but as Jesus said, *"...born of the spirit..." (John 3:6)*. The outward man remains the same as it was prior to new birth. The inward man changes radically, it becomes *"...a new creation; old things have passed away; behold, all thing have become new..." (II Corinthians 5:17)*.

Rewards of Heavenly Submission

Paul described the effects of the inward spiritual changes made in everyone who is *"...baptized into Christ..."* in easily understandable terms in his letter to the church at Galatia.

> *"For you are all sons of God through faith in Christ Jesus. For as many of you as were baptized into Christ have put on Christ. There is neither Jew nor Greek, there is neither slave nor free, there is neither male nor female; for you are all one in Christ Jesus."* **Galatians 3:26-29**

The contrast in terms *"...neither Jew nor Greek...slave nor free...male nor female..."* are contrasts defining the outward natural parts of mankind. When a person is born again, his outward natural part is *not* changed; his inward spiritual part is changed. Every born again person is spiritually a new creation, but naturally they remain the same as their natural birth made them, *"...Jew or Greek...slave or free...male or female..."*. Men and women do not stop being men and women simply because they are born again. **The distinction between natural and spiritual is pivotal as foundation upon which to base understanding of submission in marriage!**

Paul wrote extensively on the subject of marriage, either addressing issues in marriages in the churches or comparing marriage to the church. In his letter to the church at Ephesus he wrote...

> *"Wives submit to your own husbands, as to the Lord. For the husband is head of the wife, as also Christ is head of the church; and He is the Savior of the body. Therefore, just as the church is subject to Christ, so let the wives be to their own husbands in everything. Husbands, love your wives, just as Christ also loved the church and gave Himself for her, that He might sanctify and cleanse her with the washing*

Submission in Marriage

of water by the word, that He might present her to Himself a glorious church, not having spot or wrinkle or any such thing, but that she should be holy and without blemish. So husbands ought to love their own wives as their own bodies; he who loves his wife loves himself. For no one ever hated his own flesh, but nourishes and cherishes it, just as the Lord does the church. For we are members of His body, of His flesh and of His bones. For this reason a man shall leave his father and mother and be joined to his wife, and the two shall become one flesh. This is a great mystery, but I speak concerning Christ and the church. Nevertheless let each one of you in particular so love his own wife as himself, and let the wife see that she respects her husband."
Ephesians 5:22-33

Some revelations about which Paul wrote in this portion of Scripture by inspiration of God the Holy Spirit are unequivocal.

1. *"Wives submit to your own husbands, as to the Lord."*

2. *"For the husband is head of the wife, as also Christ is head of the church; and He is the Savior of the body."*

3. *"Therefore, just as the church is subject to Christ, so let the wives be to their own husbands in everything."*

Understanding of these statements must conform to the standard of Christ or a wrong result will ensue. Scripture has already revealed God's design for marriage is for a man and a woman to become a husband and a wife *(Genesis 2:21-25)*. Since it was God the Holy Spirit who inspired Paul to write *Ephesians 5:22-33* and since there is no Scriptural amendment to God's design for marriage, it is accurate to understand the terms *"...husbands, wives, and marriage..."* according to God's original design.

Paul's use of the terms *"...husband..."* and *"...wife..."* define roles based on outward, temporary, and natural, as opposed to inward, eternal, and spiritual. **The husband is head of his own wife in the natural role of husband and wife only!**

Consider a natural illustration:

Within a marriage a husband's wife is a dentist. The husband develops an abscessed tooth. He enters his wife's dental office for treatment. The moment this husband enters his wife's dental practice a significant change in roles is required.

The husband's wife does not stop being his wife, but she must function in another role in relation to her husband. She must function as a professional dentist in order to apply her training to help this man who also happens to be her husband. According to Scripture, *"...wives submit to your own husband..."* because *"...the husband is the head of the wife..."* and she is to be *"...subject...to (her) own husband in everything..."*. Inaccurate understanding of these unequivocal statements will produce disastrous results in this dental illustration.

The husband in this illustration has no dental training. He does not exercise *"...headship..."* over the woman dentist simply because she is his wife. He is not required to go to his wife for treatment. However, if he chooses to go to her, he must willingly submit to her as *"...dentist..."* as she labors to apply her dental training on his behalf.

Submission in Marriage

There are many such illustrations which could be given, but the point is clear in the dental illustration. Two individuals can have a diversity of roles each role changing the basis for them to relate to one another: Husband to wife, man to dentist, father to mother of their children, and so on. The roles can be many and diverse for both husband and wife. Scripture states, *"...wives submit to your own husband..."* because *"...the husband is the head of the wife..."* and she is to be *"...subject...to (her) own husband in everything..."*. However, husband and wife are only two roles a man and woman can have in a marriage relationship as we have already seen in the dental illustration. The husband is the head of his own wife but not head of the woman functioning as a dentist who also happens to be his wife. Simple!

One other consideration must be made regarding the unequivocal revelations about which Paul wrote in his letter to the church at Ephesus. *"Therefore, just as the church is subject to Christ, so let the wives be to their own husbands in everything."* Scripture presented the will of God regarding submission to governing authorities in the context of the apostles before the Sanhedrin Council.

> *"... 'Did we not strictly command you not to teach in this name? And look, you have filled Jerusalem with your doctrine, and intend to bring this Man's blood on us!' But Peter and the other apostles answered and said: **We ought to obey God rather than men**..." Acts 5:28-42*

The governing authorities of the kingdom of God are always priority over the governing authorities of any other kingdom!

Rewards of Heavenly Submission

This understanding applies to the husband being the head of his own wife. *"Therefore, just as the church is subject to Christ, so let the wives be to their own husbands in everything."* is the will of God as long as the husband's *"...headship..."* does not violate the governing authority of the kingdom of God. Absolutely no governing authority has priority over God and the governing authorities of His kingdom! If a wife's own husband asks her to do something which is in violation to the governing authorities of God and His kingdom, she is to remain submitted to God!

The roles of *"...husband and wife..."* are restricted to temporal outward conditions of man and woman here in the natural world. There are no marriages in heaven.

> *"The same day the Sadducees, who say there is no resurrection, came to Him and asked Him, saying: 'Teacher, Moses said that if a man dies, having no children, his brother shall marry his wife and raise up offspring for his brother. Now there were with us seven brothers. The first died after he had married, and having no offspring, left his wife to his brother. Likewise the second also, and the third, even to the seventh. Last of all the woman died also. Therefore, in the resurrection, whose wife of the seven will she be? For they all had her." Jesus answered and said to them, 'You are mistaken, not knowing the Scriptures nor the power of God. For in the resurrection they neither marry nor are given in marriage, but are like angels of God in heaven. But concerning the resurrection of the dead, have you not read what was spoken to you by God, saying, 'I am the God of Abraham, the God of Isaac, and the God of Jacob'? God is not the God of the dead, but of the living." And when the multitudes heard this, they were astonished at His teaching."* **Matthew 22:23-33** *(Also found in* **Mark 12:18-27** *and* **Luke 20:27-40)**

Submission in Marriage

In Christ there are *"...no Jews nor Greeks, no slaves nor free, no males nor females..." (Galatians 3:26-29)*; everyone is one in Christ. The husband as head over his wife does not apply in the spirit in Christ because there are no males and females in Christ. There is no indirect relationship anyone has with Jesus as Lord which must pass through another person to get to Jesus. Everyone who is born again has direct and immediate access to Jesus.

Even though it is the will of God for the *"...husband to be the head of his own wife..."*, the husband is not to *"...lord..."* over his wife. The husband *"...is head of the wife, as also Christ is head of the church..."*. Even though Jesus is Lord, He does not *"...lord..."* over the members of His own body, as **Strong's Exhaustive Concordance of the Bible** defined *"...lord..." (2634)*.

> *2634 katakurieno* from *2596* and *2601; to lord against*, i.e. *control, subjugate*: -- exercise dominion over (lordship), be lord over, overcome.

Jesus does not *"...exercise dominion over..."* us. Peter admonished the elders who oversee the flock of God not to do so as *"...lords over those entrusted to you..." (I Peter 5:1-5)* and neither are husbands to *"...control or subjugate...."* their wives. **Submission in the new covenant is always from a willing heart!**

This opens the door to a really important question: What causes a wife to submit to her husband with a willing heart? Of course, the number one priority is because it is Jesus' will. However, even this requires a willing heart.

Rewards of Heavenly Submission

People willingly submit to Jesus because they see Him as He really is. Scripture has already established *"...the husband is the head of the wife, as also Christ is head of the church..."*. In other words, the husband is to be head of his wife like Christ is the head of the church. Paul provided revelation in **Ephesians 5:22-33** *"...**how**..."* Christ fulfills His role as head of the church: *"...He loves the church, gave Himself for the church, nourishes and cherishes the church..."*. God the Holy Spirit inspired Paul to write husbands are to *"...love your wives, just as Christ also loved the church..."*. He continues with, *"...husbands ought to love their own wives as their own bodies; he who loves his wife loves himself. For no one ever hated his own flesh, but nourishes and cherishes it..."*.

This revelation regarding *"...how..."* a husband is to fulfill his role as head of his wife provides great motivation for his wife to desire to submit to him with a willing heart: *She sees her husband's love for her, how he gives himself for her, how he nourishes and cherishes her.* If the husband follows the way of the Lord for his role as husband, it will create a condition conducive for his wife to *"...desire..."* to submit to him. However, his actions will not guarantee his wife will submit. Jesus loved the world so much He gave His life for us, but many refuse to submit to Him as Lord. The husband must not follow the way of the Lord as the means to get his wife to submit but rather because **his heart is submitted to the Lord**, and he desires the way of the Lord as the way **he** lives.

Submission in Marriage

Marriage is a type of relationship!

"Relationships can only be successfully developed through effective communication. Effective communication is only possible by properly identifying roles. Roles are the foundation for effective communication. Effective communication is the foundation for healthy relationships."
Chapter Five, page 48

If we apply this relationship model to marriage, we understand the *"...roles..."* of husband and wife are foundational for how a man and woman communicate with one another in their marriage. When a man receives revelation that his *"...role..."* as husband is to be fulfilled like Christ fulfills His *"...role..."* as Head of the church, he must choose whether he will follow Christ as His pattern, or not. His communication with his wife is founded on his understanding of his *"...role..."* as husband.

Scripture speaks very clearly regarding husbands: *"...love your wives, just as Christ also loved the church..."*, *"...husbands ought to love their own wives as their own bodies; he who loves his wife loves himself. For no one ever hated his own flesh, but nourishes and cherishes it..."*. A man fulfilling his *"...role..."* as husband is to communicate with his wife in a *"...loving, nourishing, and cherishing..."* manner. This form of communication is the will of God designed to be the foundation upon which a marriage relationship can be built healthy and prosperous.

What is expected of the woman in her role as wife? Most of the revelation contained in ***Ephesians 5:22-33*** addresses the man in his *"...role..."* as husband. Only **verse 22**, *"Wives submit (5293)* *to your own husbands, as to the Lord....*" and the last half of *verse 33*, "*...let the wife see that she respects (5399) her husband...*" provide instructions to the wife. In *Chapter One, page 3,* we included definition from **Strong's Exhaustive Concordance of the Bible** of the Greek term *5293 hupotasso* for which the English term "*...submit...*" is translated.

> *5293 hupotasso* from *5259* and *5021*; to *subordinate*; reflex. to *obey*: -- be under obedience (obedient), put under, subdue unto, (be, make) subject (to, unto), be (put) in subjection (to, under), submit self unto.

God expects a man's wife to "*...submit...*" herself to her "*...own husband...*". Referring again to *Chapter One, page three*, we established a simple definition of "*...submission...*" in the church as "*...a person's willingness to yield to the rule of Christ...*". A wife's submission to her own husband then is her willingness to yield to the rule of her husband: "*...Wives submit to your own husbands, as to the Lord...*" **Ephesians 5:22**.

Marriage relationships of husbands and wives are compared to Christ and the church. The way submission is designed to work between Christ and the church is the pattern for submission between husbands and wives.

> "Until the dispensation changes no aspect of Jesus' "*...rule over men...*" involves "*...a rod of iron...*" and **never** involves subtle and crafty enticements in any dispensation. Although Jesus is... over...all men, He has chosen not to exert "*...control...*" over men. Nor does He seduce men with enticements designed to allure them into His rule. In order for Jesus to rule men, men must "*...submit...*" to Him based on their knowledge of Him!"
> **Chapter One, page 2**

Submission in Marriage

"Wives submit to their own husbands..." must be done as an act of faith out of the abundance of the heart. This understanding is essential as the foundation for healthy submission in the marriage. The husband is not to *"...subjugate..."* his wife. That is, he must nor force his wife to submit in any way, not even quoting Scripture, declaring *"...it is the will of God...".* She must submit freely, gladly, and willingly.

What is the meaning of *"...let the wife see that she respects (5399) her husband..."*? **Strong's Exhaustive Concordance of the Bible** defines *5399* as:

> *5399 phobeo* from *5401*; to *frighten*, i.e. (pass.) to *be alarmed*; by anal. to *be in awe* of, i.e. *revere*: -- be (+ sore) afraid, fear (exceedingly), reverence.

The same Greek term *5399* used in *Ephesians 5:33* regarding God's expectations for the wife toward her husband was used in the context of King Herod and John the Baptist: *"...Herod feared (5399) John..." (Mark 6:20).* Through a strange series of events in order for King Herod to keep his oath given to Herodias' daughter *"...sent an executioner and commanded his (John's) head..." (Mark 6:27).* Whatever type of *"...fear..." (5399)* Herod had for John, it was not fear that John would do harm to him as King nor as a man. The same verse, *Mark 6:20* from which it is written *"...Herod feared John..."* it is also written *"...Herod feared John, knowing that he was a just and holy man...".* Herod's *"...fear..."* of John was *"...reverence..."* because Herod knew John to be *"...a just and holy man...".*

Rewards of Heavenly Submission

In order to understand marriage relationships, a very specific revelation is required: Marriage, designed by God, was never intended to function properly without God! ***Ephesians 5:22-33*** is the will of God for marriages ***in the Lord!*** The moment Adam sinned; he partook of death and was separated from the life of God! These conditions not only affected him as an individual, they affected Eve and their marriage. They had a marriage without God. People without Christ today are not only *"...lost..."* as individuals, their marriages are without God, too. **Marriages were designed to include God!**

The *"...reverence..."* a wife is to have for *"...her husband..."* is designed to be founded on her husband being the *"...righteousness of God in Christ Jesus..."*! King Herod based his *"...reverence..."* for John the Baptist on John being *"...a just and holy man..."*. How much more is *"...reverence..."* due a husband who has *"...become the righteousness of God in Him (Christ Jesus)..."* ***(II Corinthians 5:21)***.

Of course a wife in Christ has *"...become the righteousness of God in Him (Christ Jesus)..."*, too. Such *"...reverence..."* is not based on the outward *"...male or female..."* but by being *"...one in Christ..."*. However, God the Holy Spirit inspired Paul to use the term *"...respect / reverence..."* (Greek term **5399**) as the expectation of God for the *"...wife..."* in relation to her *"...husband..."*. These are roles applicable to the outward temporary man.

Submission in marriage has been easily corrupted for at least two really powerful reasons: Marriage, designed by God, was never intended to function properly without God!

Submission in Marriage

And, *"...righteousness..."* was given to us to become the way we live, not just a teaching we received. If we can restore these two foundational revelations back into the church we will see submission in marriage restored, too!

Rewards of Heavenly Submission

Conclusion

Jesus gave a simple contrast between Himself and *"...the thief..."* which is to serve as a foundational premise for the entirety of our lives in His kingdom...

> *"...The thief does not come except to steal, and to kill, and to destroy. I have come that they may have life, and that they may have it more abundantly..."* **John 10:10**

John was inspired to present this same contrast...

> *"...Little children, it is the last hour; and as you have heard that the Antichrist is coming, even now many antichrists have come, by which we know that it is the last hour. They went out from us, but they were not of us; for if they had been of us, they would have continued with us; but they went out that they might be made manifest, that none of them were of us. But you have an anointing from the Holy One, and you know all things. I have not written to you because you do not know the truth, but because you know it, and that no lie is of the truth. Who is a liar but he who denies that Jesus is the Christ? He is antichrist who denies the Father and the Son. Whoever denies the Son does not have the Father either; he who acknowledges the Son has the Father also. Therefore let that abide in you which you heard from the beginning. If what you heard from the beginning abides in you, you also will abide in the Son and in the Father. And this is the promise that He has promised us -- eternal life. These things I have written to you concerning those who try to deceive you. But the anointing which you have received from Him abides in you, and you do not need that anyone teach you; but as the same anointing teaches you concerning all things, and is true, and is not a lie, and just as it has taught you, you will abide in Him."* **I John 2:18-27**

Rewards of Heavenly Submission

Peter was inspired to admonish the church on this very subject...

*"...Be sober, be vigilant; because your adversary the devil walks about like a roaring lion, seeking whom he may devour..." **I Peter 5:8***

Paul was inspired to present this understanding in a peculiar manner...

*"...Oh, that you would bear with me in a little folly -- and indeed you do bear with me. For I am jealous for you with godly jealousy. For I have betrothed you to one husband, that I may present you as a chaste virgin to Christ. But I fear, lest somehow, as the serpent deceived Eve by his craftiness, so your minds may be corrupted from the simplicity that is in Christ." **II Corinthians 11:1-3***

Whether Jesus' archenemy is referred to as *"...the thief..."*, *"...the devil..."*, *"...the Antichrist..."*, or *"...the serpent..."* it is clear he is *"...**anti-Christ**..."!* Because Jesus cannot *"...rule..."* men in this dispensation unless they willingly submit to Him, it is understandable why the enemy attacks the revelation of *"...submission..."* with such violence: *He does not want men to submit to Jesus!*

The revelation of *"...submission..."* has been so difficult to communicate, understand, and embrace because of the devices of the enemy sent to deceive and to steal what the Lord has given as holy provision in His kingdom. Because the beautiful revelation of *"...submission..."* is straight from the heart of Abba, our Father, it should be a delight to our heart!

Conclusion

If we will turn our hearts toward the Lord, the Holy Spirit will provide us with spiritual sight to see *"...submission..."* from God's perspective. Once the revelation of *"...submission..."* is presented in an anointed accurate manner to a person whose heart is turned toward the Lord, it will open the door for the person to see with his spiritual eye what his natural eye could not see. Holy Spirit inspired sight ought not to be resisted. Any person who resists sight provided by God the Holy Spirit is proud, lacking humility.

'God resists the proud, but gives grace to the humble.'

"Therefore submit to God. Resist the devil and he will flee from you." **James 4:6,7**

***Heavenly submission
will activate divine power
causing "...the devil..." to flee from us!***

---

www.ingramcontent.com/pod-product-compliance
Lightning Source LLC
Chambersburg PA
CBHW071307040426
42444CB00009B/1914